D0915577

THE POWER OF
ACCOUNTABILITY

STUDIES IN GOVERNMENT
AND PUBLIC POLICY

THE POWER OF ACCOUNTABILITY

Offices of Inspector General at
the State and Local Levels

Robin J. Kempf

 University Press of Kansas

© 2020 by the University Press of Kansas
All rights reserved

Published by the University Press of Kansas (Lawrence, Kansas 66045), which was
organized by the Kansas Board of Regents and is operated and funded by Emporia
State University, Fort Hays State University, Kansas State University, Pittsburg State
University, the University of Kansas, and Wichita State University

Library of Congress Cataloging-in-Publication Data

Names: Kempf, Robin J., author.
Title: The power of accountability : offices of inspector general at the state and local
levels / Robin J. Kempf.
Description: Lawrence : University Press of Kansas, 2020. | Series: Studies in
government and public policy | Includes bibliographical references and index. |
Identifiers: LCCN 2019025717
    ISBN 9780700628971 (cloth)
    ISBN 9780700628988 (epub)
Subjects: LCSH: Government accountability—United States. | Government
Investigators—United States.
Classification: LCC JF1525.A26 K46 2020 | DDC 352.8/82130973—dc23
LC record available at https://lccn.loc.gov/2019025717.

Printed in the United States of America

10 9 8 7 6 5 4 3 2 1

The paper used in this publication is recycled and contains 30 percent postconsumer
waste. It is acid free and meets the minimum requirements of the American National
Standard for Permanence of Paper for Printed Library Materials Z39.48-1992.

This book is dedicated to Peter H. and Alison K. H.

CONTENTS

FIGURES AND TABLES

FIGURES

TABLES

ACKNOWLEDGMENTS

I started thinking about this book years before I started writing it. I was working as an attorney with the state of Kansas when I was honored to be appointed the inaugural Inspector General for the now-nonexistent Kansas Health Policy Authority. Fairly quickly thereafter, I was overwhelmed with the responsibility of establishing an oversight entity into an agency that was not truly interested in having increased oversight. After a year of intense politicking to establish the independent role of the Office of Inspector General (OIG) and launch its activities, I found I had thrown my back out, my hair was both turning gray and falling out, I'd developed insomnia, and my doctor was threatening a diagnosis of irritable bowel syndrome. I stepped away from the position that *may* have been too stressful for me.

Despite this, dare I say, negative experience, I had become fascinated with how we pursue accountability in this country. In particular, I wanted to study OIGs. Why had this specific method of achieving accountability caught the imagination of many policymakers across the country? And given my challenging experience, could OIGs truly make a difference? I entered the University of Kansas School of Public Policy and Administration to study just that.

This book, which grew from an experience into an idea into a dissertation and finally into the book you have before you, would not have happened without inspectors general (IGs) around the country willing to teach me about their experiences. I thank each of the IGs and deputy IGs who gave me their time and directed me to relevant documents about their offices. I also thank the Association of Inspectors General for providing me Certified Inspector General training and providing multiple venues where I could be immersed in the field and network with other OIG practitioners.

I wholeheartedly congratulate the OIG staff across the country for working diligently to report on the activities of our government and the expenditure of our tax dollars. This is hard but important work. I wish you continued fortitude as you pursue your mission of government accountability.

I thank my classmates at the University of Kansas and my colleagues at John Jay College of Criminal Justice for their support and encouragement. I also want to thank my editor at the University Press of Kansas, David Congdon, for taking a chance on me. I give special thanks to Dr. Chuck Epp for his guidance and mentorship. Chuck has always gone the extra mile to support my academic efforts, whether through the discussion of theory, editing of chapters, or introductions to book publishers. It is greatly appreciated. I would go so far to say that I would like to be just like Chuck when I grow up. Thanks to Evan Luskin for additional editing help. Finally, thanks to my parents and role models, Andrea Kempf and George Kempf, for being two of the smartest people I have ever known, and to my husband, Peter Haxton, and our daughter, Alison Kempf-Haxton, for making it all worth it.

THE POWER OF
ACCOUNTABILITY

1. The Idea of an Office of Inspector General

Cook County's chief watchdog has concluded that more than $330,000 in property tax breaks and refunds that [Illinois] Democratic gubernatorial candidate J. B. Pritzker received on one of his Gold Coast mansions—in part by removing toilets—constituted a "scheme to defraud." Cook County Inspector General Patrick Blanchard also recommends in the confidential report that Cook County should try to recover the money from the billionaire. . . . The bombshell report comes just weeks ahead of a contentious November election, with polls showing Pritzker ahead by double digits.

> —Tina Sfondeles, *"Game of Thrones? Watchdog Sees 'Scheme to Defraud'*
> *[in Illinois Gubernatorial Candidate] Pritzker's Toilet Tax Break,"*
> Chicago Sun-Times, *October 1, 2018*

The chairman of the board of Baltimore's Employee Retirement System [Jerome Sanders] has been removed and its chief investment officer [Eliot Powell] is out of a job amid an inquiry that found they had an undisclosed business relationship of more than 30 years, according to an inspector general's report Thursday and city officials. The report said the board chairman recruited the executive to the post overseeing investments for the $1.6 billion system that administers the plans of more than 18,000 current and former city employees. . . . Once he got the job in December, Powell didn't show up for work most of the time and tried to steer $15 million in the system's funds to an investment firm where he had personal investments, the report said.

> —Ian Duncan, *"Report: Baltimore Retirement Fund Board Chair Recruited Business*
> *Partner to Oversee $1.6 Billion in Investments,"* Baltimore Sun, *October 4, 2018*

Offices of inspector general make headlines across the country. As the examples above illustrate, these offices are energetic engines of accountability at the state and local levels of government in the United States. Yet offices of inspector general (hereinafter "OIGs") are a relatively new phenomenon. Virtually none existed before 1976, but today there are 73 OIGs in the federal government and 170 at both the state and local levels.[1] Fully two-thirds of the states have at least one OIG. The widespread adoption of the OIG model is an important development in the transformation of systems of governmental accountability in the United States.

What are OIGs? Why have they been so widely adopted, and what do they

1

do? In what ways do they contribute to accountability, and what are the limitations of their contribution? Although several excellent studies have analyzed OIGs at the federal level,[2] none have examined the vastly larger and more varied body of state and local OIGs. This book sets out to address these questions with empirical data on all state and local OIGs. It focuses on the spread of the OIG concept across state and local levels of government and the conflicts that have led to variations in the design and implementation of these agencies. In doing so, it explores the power of what I will call the inspector general idea: an institutional model of how to keep subnational governmental units accountable to the public.

The research is based on a thorough identification of state and local OIGs through a review of government websites, laws, and ordinances, followed by original surveys of the identified OIGs. To add depth to survey data, this book relies on interviews with thirty-eight OIG staff in eight states. In addition, it draws on a review of legislative history and media reports in two states that had created an OIG but subsequently abolished it. This research results in a description of three phases that make up the creation of a state or local OIG: conceptualization, design, and implementation.

Throughout these phases we will see the power of the aspiration for accountability. Americans expect government officials to be accountable for their policies and actions. Many have become increasingly disenchanted with conventional means for achieving accountability. OIGs appear to many people to be able to fill the accountability gap. This aspiration for a new and more effective mechanism of accountability motivates citizens and policymakers to propose adopting an OIG, it informs the intense politics of designing these offices, and it propels efforts to meaningfully implement these new oversight mechanisms. This book aims to show how this powerful aspiration has propelled OIGs to the forefront of efforts to achieve governmental accountability, and how putting it into practice is inevitably complicated by political disagreement and contrasting ideas about what is necessary to make it work. First, though, we must understand what an OIG is.

OIG OVERVIEW

An OIG is a bureaucratic unit dedicated to government accountability. OIGs are typically set up to oversee a particular government agency (or, sometimes, several agencies). Commonly, OIGs are independent of the agencies they are charged with overseeing, so that their oversight is not controlled by the agency being overseen. (As we shall see, state and local OIGs vary considerably in this degree of independence.) An OIG provides accountability by monitoring the agency or agencies under its jurisdiction and producing reports about agency programs and operations, identifying problems, and making recommendations for fixing these problems. An OIG's jurisdiction usually extends beyond monitoring the actions of public employees to include the actions of public contractors and beneficiaries of public programs. Monitoring and reporting come in the form of audits and/or investigations. Often audits and investigations are initiated in response to complaints about the agency or agencies that the OIG oversees, but most OIGs also investigate or audit issues that are deemed problematic according to their discretion. Although OIGs commonly have broad powers of investigation and audit, they typically have no authority to prosecute criminal behavior or to require changes in the agency being overseen. Put simply, their authority is limited to monitoring, reporting, and referring. If changes are to occur in response to problems identified by the OIG, others—the governor, legislature, mayor, or some other official—must order them.

OIGs have proliferated across the country. Since the creation of the first modern civilian OIG on the federal level in 1976, OIGs have been established across the country and throughout all levels of government. Further, thirty-four states have established at least one OIG in an agency or for the state as a whole. Many large cities, such as New Orleans, Chicago, and Albuquerque, and counties, including Miami-Dade County, Florida; Cuyahoga County, Ohio; and Montgomery County, Maryland, have also followed suit. OIGs can also be found in school districts and sheriff's offices. Although these OIGs are not identical in structure, each of these jurisdictions has purposely established an office headed by an individual with the title of "inspector general," giving it a mission to pursue government accountability by collecting information about the actions of government employees or the use of governmental funds.

Although OIGs have been found in the military context since the days of George Washington, the first modern civilian OIG was established by Congress in 1976 to oversee the Department of Health, Education, and Welfare (HEW);[3] however, it is worth noting that this OIG was preceded in 1959 by an "Inspector General and Comptroller" for the International Cooperation Administration,[4] which might be considered the forerunner of the modern OIG.[5] The Inspector General and Comptroller performed and coordinated audits of the agency and reported its findings to Congress. Yet, the Inspector General and Comptroller was generally considered a failure due to politicization and apathy, and it was abolished in the mid-1970s.[6] The HEW OIG, on the other hand, spawned a system of federal OIGs, as it was followed by a second OIG in the Department of Energy in 1977, and by the passage of the IG

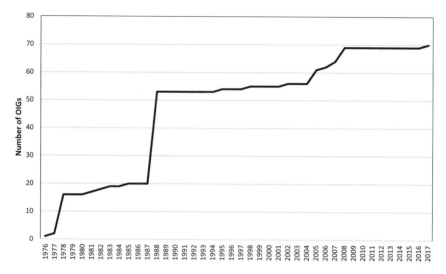

Figure 1.1. Line Chart Showing Cumulative Number of Federal OIGs, 1976–2017

Act of 1978, which placed OIGs in twelve agencies, including HEW and Energy. Here, Congress combined preexisting audit and investigation units into a single independent office and directed them to pursue issues of economy and efficiency, fraud, and abuse.

Figure 1.1 shows the growth of the number of OIGs on the federal level since 1978.[7] This figure shows a sharp increase in the number of OIGs in the year 1978 with the passage of the IG Act, and in the year 1988 with the passage of amendments to the IG Act, which created thirty-three new OIGs for regulatory agencies. After 1988, the number of federal OIGs has increased steadily and, since 2005, at an accelerated rate. Some of the most recently established OIGs have jurisdictions that cross federal agencies, including the Office of the Special Inspector General for Afghanistan Reconstruction (SIGAR) and the Office of the Special Inspector General for the Troubled Asset Relief Program (SIGTARP), both formed in 2008.

This growing sector of OIGs in the federal government have drawn the attention of social scientists, who have explored their creation and structure,[8] the evolution of their activities over time,[9] the impact of their activities on agencies that they oversee,[10] and strategies they use to develop relationships with stakeholders.[11] These scholars have overlooked that while the number of OIGs grew on the federal level, states and local governments, too, began to create OIGs. Figure 1.2 shows the growth of state and local OIGs since 1975. Subnational OIGs were identified through an extensive review of govern-

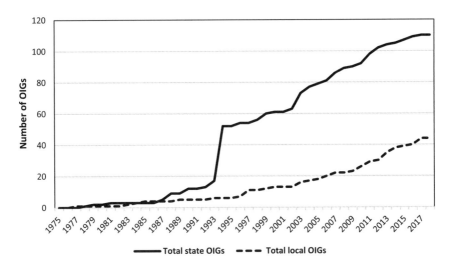

Figure 1.2. Line Chart Showing Cumulative Number of State and Local OIGs, 1976–2018

ment websites, and state and local statutes or ordinances, as well as multiple searches on the internet using different search engines. The date of the creation of the OIG was collected through a review of the same sources coupled with electronic and telephonic surveys. This research identified all state and local OIGs in existence at the beginning of 2018 that either had an internet presence or were referred to in online public government documents or news articles. (Data for twelve OIGs were not available.) Any OIGs that had been created after 1975 but no longer existed in 2018 are not included here.

Figure 1.2 shows a large jump in the number of state OIGs in 1994 resulting from the enactment of the Florida OIG Act, which placed an OIG in every state agency. Apart from that big jump, there has been a relatively steady and ongoing increase in adoption of OIGs at the state and local levels. The average annual growth rate for local OIGs over the thirty-year period of 1975 to 2015 was 10.6 percent. The average annual growth rate for state OIGs for the same time period was 16.6 percent. Today, there are 118 state-level OIGs, 49 local OIGs (including Washington, DC), and 3 multijurisdictional OIGs. These multijurisdictional OIGs include the Delaware River Port Authority, the Port Authority of New York & New Jersey, and the Washington Metropolitan Area Transit Authority. The total number of local and state OIGs, including the multijurisdictional OIGs, is 170, more than twice the number of OIGs on the federal level.[12]

In the past decades OIGs have spread widely across most regions of the

Table 1.1. Number of State-Level and Local OIGs by Region and State

Region/State	Total state-level OIGs	Total local OIGs	Total OIGs
New England			
Connecticut	0	0	0
Maine	0	0	0
Massachusetts	1	0	1
New Hampshire	0	0	0
Rhode Island	0	0	0
Vermont	0	0	0
Mid-Atlantic			
New Jersey	1	1	2
New York	8	3	11
Pennsylvania	1	2	3
East North Central			
Illinois	11	9	20
Indiana	1	0	1
Michigan	1	2	3
Ohio	2	2	4
Wisconsin	2	0	2
West North Central			
Iowa	0	0	0
Kansas	3	0	3
Minnesota	1	0	1
Missouri	1	0	1
Nebraska	2	0	2
North Dakota	0	0	0
South Dakota	0	0	0
South Atlantic			
Delaware	0	0	0
Florida	38	14	52
Georgia	5	0	5
Maryland	3	4	7
North Carolina	1	0	1
South Carolina	3	0	3
Virginia	1	1	2
District of Columbia	0	1	1
West Virginia	2	0	2
East South Central			
Alabama	1	0	1
Kentucky	4	1	5
Mississippi	0	0	0
Tennessee	2	0	2
West South Central			
Arkansas	1	0	1
Louisiana	1	2	3

Oklahoma	3	0	3
Texas	4	1	5
Mountain			
Arizona	5	0	5
Colorado	1	0	1
Idaho	0	0	0
Montana	0	0	0
Nevada	1	0	1
New Mexico	2	1	3
Utah	1	0	1
Wyoming	0	0	0
Pacific			
Alaska	0	0	0
California	3	5	8
Hawaii	0	0	0
Oregon	1	0	1
Washington	0	0	0
Multijurisdictional OIGs	3	0	0
Totals	121	49	170

Source: Author's research.

country. As of the beginning of 2018, thirty-four states and Washington, DC, had at least one OIG. Table 1.1 shows OIGs adopted by state on the state and local levels. The table demonstrates that New York, Illinois, and Florida are the leaders in OIG adoption. In addition, some regions, such as the New England and West North Central regions, have not followed the lead of the rest of the county in adopting OIGs.

THE DEMAND FOR ACCOUNTABILITY EMERGES IN THE FORM OF THE OIG

Governmental accountability is a fundamental expectation in democratic systems. At this expectation's core is the norm that those who exercise authority must be prepared to reveal and explain their official actions to the citizens they serve. As Mark Bovens observed, "Accountability is a relationship between an actor and a forum, in which the actor has an obligation to explain and to justify his or her conduct, the forum can pose questions and pass judgment, and the actor may face consequences."[13] In democratic systems, the actor is a government official, and the forum is made up of the citizens. In Western democracies, the most basic form of accountability is popular elections, in which officials explain their past actions and their intentions for the future, and the voting public passes judgment in the form of voting. Thus, while acknowledging the many complicated practical questions of how well electoral accountability works, periodic elections remain the primary means of accountability for elected officials.

Employees in the executive branch, however, are not subject to such elections by design. These employees are sheltered from reelection concerns so that they can conduct their jobs professionally, exercising expert knowledge without fear of direct political reprisal.[14] Still, democratic ideals demand that even these officials must be somehow accountable to the public, even if not directly through electoral control.[15] The most common forms of bureaucratic accountability consist of various forms of oversight by elected officials: executive appointment and directives, legislative committee hearings, legislation mandating administrative processes, budgetary controls, and ad hoc inquiries by individual elected officials. Still, especially in the post-Watergate era, many members of the public and elected officials alike have come to believe that these traditional means of accountability are not enough.

OIGs are an expression of the desire to institutionalize accountability in a new, quasibureaucratic way by trying to ensure, via oversight by independent experts, that executive branch employees are made to explain and justify their conduct and be answerable for their actions. An OIG plays an intermediary role between elected officials and the bureaucracy. Deputized by elected officials, an OIG provides independent monitoring of governmental actors and reports the results of this monitoring to those officials. The OIG does not have the authority to compel either the government actor or the entities receiving the OIG's reports to act, but it helps provide accountability through its regular monitoring and reporting.[16]

An OIG clearly is not the only way to pursue government accountability. In fact, the norm of accountability finds expression in a wide variety of institutional mechanisms, including, as noted above, legislative oversight[17] and professional standards.[18] Romzek and Dubnick explain how public employees come to be subject to a variety of accountability mechanisms, including from their bureaucratic superiors, their professional networks, applicable laws and regulations, and political pressures.[19] Prosecutors investigate and bring legal charges to punish illegal acts, and financial auditors help ensure the fiscal integrity of government operations. The pubic also sets informal expectations for the conduct of public employees.[20] The rapid spread of OIGs amidst this already-broad set of other mechanisms of accountability is best understood in the context of what Dubnick and O'Brien called the American public's "obsession" with accountability.[21]

The OIG model emerged as the accepted solution to perceived accountability problems only relatively recently. Although OIGs are as old as the country itself, the first OIG having been adopted in 1777 when General George Washington asked Congress to create an inspector general position to provide oversight of the revolutionary army's training, discipline, and treatment of soldiers, the origins of the widespread adoption of OIGs can be dated to the post-Watergate period.[22] President Richard Nixon's resignation in 1974 following the Watergate scandal initiated ongoing concern about a deficit of accountability in the executive branch.[23] This concern shows little sign of abating in the context of long-term decline in trust in government and repeated exposure of large corruption scandals, such as the conviction of former Illinois governor Rod Blagojevich (resulting in a fourteen-year sentence), the conviction of former Virginia governor Bob McDonnell (whose conviction was overturned on appeal to the Supreme Court), and the "Bridgegate" scandal involving accusations of abuse of power by the former New Jersey governor Chris Christie (which resulted in several convictions of the governor's staff). These conditions have left the public and their elected officials dismayed with existing accountability mechanisms and clamoring for new, novel ways to oversee the executive and administrative arms of government.

As OIGs have spread across the nation, they have evolved from the original federal model of troop inspection. Over time, we see the emergence of a generally accepted model, or archetype, of a civilian OIG with a mandate to audit and investigate the actions of public managers and employees, government contractors, and beneficiaries of public programs. The key components of the archetype, which include the mandate to investigate individual cases of bad behavior and to make systemic recommendations to prevent bad behavior in the future, have gained a wide consensus among inspector general practitioners. This consensus on the basic contours of the OIG archetype illustrate a phenomenon of what scholars refer to as "institutionalization," or the widespread adoption of a common model or way of doing something. In the words of Philip Selznick, a practice has become institutionalized when it comes to take on "value beyond the technical requirements of the task at hand," meaning that it is viewed as the right way to do something regardless of whether it is clearly the most effective way to do it in each instance.[24] In fact, studies informed by this theory observe that in responding to broader ideas and norms, individual organizations often adopt organizational forms that are inefficient or unresponsive to local conditions.[25] Thus, institutions often "reflect the myths of their institutional environments instead of the demands of their work activities."[26]

The archetype of the OIG grew from, but has grown beyond, the original civilian OIG concept introduced on the federal level in the 1970s. As Light describes, the federal model was created to address specific concerns Congress had with several large federal agencies, such as failures of communication between investigative and audit units, but also reflected political compromises.[27]

The OIG archetype, developed by OIG practitioners to improve on the federal model and provide objective monitoring and reporting, represents a pure or ideal form. Its key components are: a statutory basis for the OIG agency, independence from the entity that the OIG oversees, and legal authority to pursue both investigations and audits. These components give the OIG autonomy to investigate and report, free from fear of censorship by the agency being overseen. This book will demonstrate the vibrancy and widespread approval of this archetype of the OIG.

This book will also show that some jurisdictions adopt deviations from the archetypal model. Sometimes these deviations are benign and simply a function of local preferences. For instance, a key element of the archetype is to have authority to conduct both *audits* (that examine issues of effectiveness and efficiency) and *investigations* (that look into allegations of fraud, waste, and abuse). This dual authority has been endorsed by the Association of Inspectors General and is part of an archetypal OIG; having the power of both investigations and audits is viewed as essential to a robust OIG. Nonetheless, while some state and local OIGs perform both audits and investigations, a significant number perform only investigations, and a few perform only audits.

Other deviations reflect a deliberate decision to remove significant powers from an OIG, despite the locality's desire for increased government accountability. For example, OIGs vary in their independence from the entities they oversee. Independence helps OIGs produce unbiased reports, as opposed to reports with contents manipulated for political reasons. On the federal level, OIG independence is protected in that an inspector general (IG) is appointed based on their professional qualifications and not according to political affiliation.[28] Additionally, many IGs are appointed by the president and confirmed by the Senate.[29] Once appointed and confirmed, the IG has full authority to manage their staff and decide which audits and investigations to pursue without interference.[30]

The archetypical state and local OIGs have these and other protections to its independence; yet, state and local OIGs may have more *or less* independence than the federal OIGs. For example, the OIG established to investigate the Cook County, Illinois, Clerk of the Circuit Court has much less independence than federal OIGs in that this IG is hired by the clerk and can be fired at will by the very agency the OIG is supposed to investigate.[31] Further, this IG reports to and is supervised by the clerk. In contrast, the Palm Beach County OIG has greater independence. In this county, the IG is not selected by any county official but by a committee made up of the local state attorney, the local public defender, and the private citizens who make up the County's Commission on Ethics.[32] Like the federal IGs, this IG must meet specified professional qualifications,[33] but unlike the federal IGs who can be removed by the president for any reason at any time, and only with notice to Congress,[34] the Palm Beach IG is appointed for a four-year term and can be removed only for cause.[35] In these ways the Palm Beach County's ordinance provides more protection of an IG's independence than the federal statutes.

OIGs also vary in the legal authority they are granted. On the federal level, OIG staff are granted law enforcement power when approved by the Department of Justice[36] and can issue subpoenas for documents.[37] These statutory powers help the OIG staff pursue the information they need for thorough investigations and audits. State and local OIGs may have more *or less* authority than federal OIGs. The Massachusetts OIG lacks law enforcement authority, but it can subpoena documents and, through a specific statutory mechanism, individuals to provide testimony.[38] The Virginia OIG has authority to subpoena both documents and testimony, and it has blanket law-enforcement authority for all its investigators.[39]

In sum, this study rests on three premises: 1) in the past several decades OIGs have been adopted widely at the state and local level, 2) practitioners in this developing field recommend an archetypal structure for these agencies that assures their authority and independence, and 3) many states and localities that have adopted OIGs incorporate significant deviations from this archetype in their OIG's design. In light of these observations, this study addresses the following three questions:

- Why are OIGs spreading so rapidly among states and localities—or *some* states and localities? As we shall see, neoinstitutional theories help explain the appeal of the OIG idea and its widespread diffusion. In brief, the OIG has emerged as a key model for how to address the perceived problem of bureaucratic accountability, and the power of this model propels its adoption in many places.

- Why do these OIGs vary so substantially in design? As we shall see, theories of policy reinvention, especially those attuned to cross-cutting political pressures in different jurisdictions, help explain why the specific form of the OIG is so different from place to place. In brief, powerful political elites sometimes push back against giving an OIG too much independence or power, producing design changes that sometimes leave an OIG in a weakened form.

- What are the implications of these variations in design for the effectiveness of OIGs as a mechanism of accountability? As we shall see, although any erosion of OIG authority and independence might be expected to undermine an OIG's effectiveness, theories of bureaucratic politics help to illuminate how, after adoption, OIG officials work strategically to gain allies and enhance their legitimacy for professional analysis so as to overcome the weaknesses of their offices' design. Although built-in design features sometimes deeply weaken an OIG, OIG officials' ongoing efforts to give life to this mechanism of accountability even in the face of great difficulty provide further evidence of the symbolic power of the OIG idea.

THE POWER OF THE "OFFICE OF INSPECTOR GENERAL" IDEA

This book will reveal three things about state and local OIGs. First, the *concept* of an office of inspector general, as an independent agency charged with overseeing a bureaucracy in order to reduce fraud, waste, abuse, ineffectiveness, and inefficiency, has gained widespread appeal. This appeal is based ultimately on the growing demand for increased government accountability based on a failure of existing accountability mechanisms. Increased accountability through constant monitoring from OIGs promises increased control, improved performance, and appropriate behavior from governmental actors through formal account-giving that provides an opportunity for decision-makers to assess and determine appropriate consequences for those governmental actors.[40]

The second element of my thesis is that while state and local elected officials find the *general* idea of an OIG appealing, some are leery of the consequences of having an office that has all of the institutional characteristics of independence and oversight that the common model demands. As a consequence, in many places the OIG as designed has been modified in key ways that reduce its effective independence and powers of oversight. As policy diffusion scholars would suggest, local and state policymakers exert their political power to reduce the policy uncertainties related to the adoption of an OIG, which results in large variation in state and local OIGs. These design variations have not developed progressively, as would be expected if jurisdictions were learning about the policy implications of an OIG from other jurisdictions. Instead, jurisdictions' unique characteristics and needs, coupled with concerns about the potential exposure of embarrassing acts, lead to the deviations in OIG structure, independence, and authority to reflect the interests of key actors.

Third, once adopted, the officials in these offices and the agencies they oversee engage in a sometimes tense contest over the implementation of oversight. The agencies overseen by OIGs chafe under this oversight and seek ways to avoid or limit it. As a result, many OIGs experience significant pushback by political actors and those who are overseen by the OIG, particularly in the early stages of implementation, which can threaten the ability of an OIG to do the job it was intended to do. In response, demonstrating another indication of the normative power of the institutional model of the OIG, OIG personnel act in ways that protect the institutional role of the OIG in the accountability process. They pursue two primary goals that sometimes conflict: to position their offices as helpful consultants, rather than as threatening "junkyard dogs," and to maintain their independence from those they monitor in order to safeguard their impartial position. To do this, inspectors general (IGs) and their staff navigate a very political environment in order to pursue government accountability. These efforts are made even though, as the accountability literature indicates, an OIG was originally conceived with a limited and early role in the accountability process.

The common thread is the strength of the norm of accountability. "Norm" in this context does not mean "typical," but rather refers to an ideal or aspirational standard. The norm of accountability (i.e., the desire to achieve accountability in government) drives the adoption of an OIG in the first place. The norm of accountability becomes embodied in an OIG, even though the resulting designs vary from place to place. Yet these OIGs are not merely symbols of accountability or institutional shells. Rather, despite efforts to narrow the OIG's ability to perform its role in supporting the accountability process, OIG staff pursue the norm of accountability by striving to improve their OIG's ability to perform its role. This is possible precisely because a shared body of knowledge has developed about how best to design these institutions.

METHODOLOGY

This study employs a mixed methods approach, using both quantitative and qualitative data to inform conclusions. The preliminary step was to identify existing state and local OIGs, as this data had not yet been compiled by any source. The OIGs were first identified in 2014 through a series of database and internet searches, including LexisNexis (looking for any state statute or regulation that mentioned an IG); state websites (such as kansas.gov); Google; Yahoo; Ask; Bing (searching for the name of the state and the term "inspector general" in the same document); the membership lists of the National Association of State Auditors, Comptrollers, and Treasurers; and of the Association of Inspectors General. This process was repeated in 2018. For each OIG, an email address was obtained.

It should be noted that each office included in the data set used the term "inspector general" in some way, but not all offices are officially titled Office of Inspector General. For example, in the data set, there is an Inspector General's Office, an Office of Inspector General Services, an Office of Legislative Inspector General, an Office of the Independent Inspector General, and the like. For the purposes of this paper, each of these offices is referred to as an OIG and the head of the OIG as an IG.[41]

My searches for OIGs yielded a universe of 170 of these units, including 118 (69 percent) at the state level, 49 (29 percent) OIGs at the local level (including Washington, DC), and 3 (2 percent) multijurisdictional OIGs. I then sought to obtain a variety of information from each of these OIGs through a combination of an online survey, using Qualtrics electronic survey software, followup telephone interviews, and a review of OIG websites. In the online survey, completed in 2014, I asked a number of questions about the offices' formation, activities, and evolution. A total of 59 OIGs responded to the survey, for an overall 37 percent response rate, comprising 42 (71 percent of 59) responses from state-level OIGs (including the OIG for Washington, DC), 16 (27 percent of 59) responses from local-level OIGs, and 1 (2 percent of 59) multijurisdictional OIG. I then supplemented the data obtained via the online survey with website reviews and telephone calls to the OIGs that had not responded to the survey. In these telephone calls I did not try to obtain all of the information addressed via the survey because the people I was able to talk with by telephone were not in a position to address the full range of the survey questions. Instead, I used the telephone survey and website review to gather basic facts about these OIGs, such as the date of their creation and their key design features. This resulted in basic information for 91 OIGs, when combined with the 55 full survey respondents, yielded data from 150 OIGs, or 94 percent of the universe. This includes 103 (69 percent of 150) state OIGs (including the OIG for Washington, DC), 44 (29 percent of 150) local OIGs, and 3 (2 percent of 150) multijurisdictional OIGs.

In addition to the data obtained from the online survey, follow-up telephone interviews, and website reviews, I conducted semi-structured interviews, both in person and on the phone, of thirty-five IGs, two deputy IGs, and one general counsel to an agency subject to OIG oversight. These interviews were conducted in eight states: Colorado, Florida, Illinois, Indiana, Louisiana, Massachusetts, Minnesota, and Virginia. The states were selected to maximize variation on key variables of levels of corruption, size of government, political culture, and OIG characteristics. I found similar patterns in states noted for high and low levels of corruption, in states with robust and well-funded bureaucracies as well as those with leaner bureaucratic establishments, in wealthy and poor states, and in more and less populated states. I am reasonably confident that these patterns are not a product of levels of corruption, the size of the bureaucracy, relative wealth, or size of population. Examples throughout the book are accompanied with a description of the state's individual characteristics to illustrate how the identified phenomena are common despite differences on these variables. Details of the sample selection can be found in appendix A.

I augmented the information obtained from each interview with a review of the following: the OIG's website, any statutory provisions and legislative history, and a review of news articles mentioning the creation of the OIG or the activities of the OIG, collected from the America's News database. I coded these documents along with the transcripts of the interviews in Atlas.ti, a qualitative analysis software.

Finally, two states, Connecticut and North Carolina, were identified, via legislative history as having adopted and subsequently repealing a state-level OIG. For these two states the legislative history of the OIG and any news reports of the OIG were collected and analyzed with Atlas.ti in order to better understand forces that stand in opposition of OIG establishment.

PLAN OF THE BOOK

In the four chapters that follow, the power of the norm of accountability is explored as it shapes the three phases of OIG adoption: conceptualization, design, and implementation. Together, these chapters offer a comprehensive analysis of the spread of the OIG concept and why variations on OIG structure emerge. The concluding chapter discusses the implications that these variations have on the goal of government accountability.

In chapter 2, the conceptualization phase, or phase I, is when the policymaker, whether legislative or executive, addresses whether an OIG is a good idea. We see that the OIG is deemed the best solution for a wide variety of problems related to perceived accountability deficits. The attractiveness of the OIG idea is best understood as an instance of what scholars call the "institutionalization" of a common model or archetype. (In fact, as chapter 3 will show, there is wide consensus among inspector general practitioners about the key elements of this archetype.) The theory of neoinstitutionalism helps explain this phenomenon. Neoinstitutionalism explores why many organizations in similar fields develop common structures and ways of doing things. The core idea is that individual organizations respond not only to local conditions but also to broader field-level ideas and norms. James G. March and Johan P. Olsen call these norms "logics of appropriateness."[42] In their description, logics of appropriateness guide individuals and organizations in how to do things, not by maximizing utility, but by acting in the right or "appropriate" way. These logics become institutionalized in rules and organizational structures.

Using this theoretical lens, this chapter explores the question: Why are OIGs spreading across states? Based on both qualitative and quantitative analyses, the chapter concludes that the spread of OIGs can be explained, to a large extent, by neoinstitutional theory. The initial impetus for creation of the first OIGs seems to have been to address a perceived practical need. Light explained that congressional motivation for the passage of the IG Act of 1978 was to address perceived deficiencies in auditing and investigations units coupled with a growing demand for information about federal agencies associated with the expansion of Congressional committees and Congressional staff that was occurring at the same time.[43] Yet, over time, the OIG has come to be less a response to a clear immediate need than a widely accepted and legitimate way to address the perceived need for greater accountability, defined broadly.

Chapter 3 focuses on phase II, the design phase, when decisions about issues regarding function, jurisdiction, authority, and independence are hammered out. The chapter explores the large variation that exists among state and local OIGs and tackles the question: Why do these OIGs vary to the extent they do? The threshold question is, however: From what do these OIGs vary? Is there a common normative model of an OIG from which variation can be measured? The answer proposed in chapter 3 is *yes*.

The first part of this chapter explores the nature of an "ideal model" or archetype of an OIG, developed through legislative experimentation on the federal level and subsequently codified in documents drafted by the Association of Inspectors General. These documents drafted by OIG practitioners represents the accepted model OIG, ideally positioned to provide independent oversight and accountability. The second part documents the widespread variation from the archetype that was found from surveys and interviews of OIG practitioners. Many of these variations are quite striking and significant in that they work to *weaken* an OIG's role in the accountability process. The final of the chapter part explores the reasons for these variations. Data from interviews show that the large variation in the design of state and local OIGs arise from differences in jurisdictions' characteristics and needs, and from concerns about giving this unit too much power. The variations shown, and the reasons for these variations, emphasize how the idea of accountability shapes OIGs. The emergence of an archetype demonstrates the desire to pursue accountability in its strongest form. Yet, the deliberate weakening of OIGs in the design phase shows concern about what accountability in the form of an OIG means.

In chapter 4, the implementation phase, or phase III, the OIG staff get to work. Once an OIG is adopted, the officials in these offices and the agencies they oversee engage in an ongoing, sometimes tense contest over the terms of oversight. Those who are subject to the OIG's oversight and their allies who oppose the OIG's presence are motivated by trepidation about accountability. Those who work for the OIG are motivated to pursue accountability. Thus, the power of the norm of accountability is often a struggle between these two parties. This struggle over implementation is the subject of chapter 4. Descriptive theories of government accountability and theories of bureaucratic politics help to explain the character of these struggles.

This chapter shows that this tension between an OIG's role in accountability and the concerns of those being overseen results in a powerful dynamic. Those who are subject to information-gathering and reporting fear the consequences, and this leads them to employ various strategies to undermine the role of an OIG in the accountability process. In particular, strategies challenge an OIG's ability to collect information and its objectivity. In contrast, OIG staff are strongly dedicated to their mission of accountability, and this results in their committed efforts to ensure they produce quality and useful work products that will have relevance in the accountability process. This dynamic is expanded upon in chapter 4, drawing from IG interviews and newspaper reports about OIG activities, and it shows that OIGs, and IGs in particular, are required to negotiate a politicized environment and develop allies to support its role and its work.

The final chapter, chapter 5, concludes with an examination of the implications for government accountability, in both policies and practice, that arise from the tensions described in chapters 2 through 4. The common thread in each of these stages, the conceptualization phase, the design phase, and the implementation phase, is the strength of the norm of accountability. This norm drives the adoption of an OIG in the first place. The norm of accountability becomes embodied in an OIG, even though the resulting designs vary from place to place. Yet, these OIGs are not merely symbols of accountability or institutional shells. Rather, despite methods to narrow the OIG's ability to perform its role in supporting the accountability process, OIG staff pursue the norm of accountability by striving to improve their OIG's ability to perform its role.

In sum, I will show that the normative ideal of accountability and the institutionalized model of an office of inspector general have driven the widespread adoption of OIGs. The particular designs of these agencies vary considerably, however, and this variation is best understood as shaped by local politics of contention over whether to have independent oversight and how much of it to have. Supporters of the OIG model strive to adopt and implement agencies that have all of the key characteristics of the OIG archetype. Opponents try to chip away at key elements of independence or investigatory authority. At the implementation stage, OIG leaders and staff prove to be especially committed to the OIG model and seek to carry out independent oversight—even when the design of their agency limits their independence or authority, or in the face of opposition from those who are being overseen. This, too, indicates the power of the normative ideal of OIG accountability. Simply put, my interpretation of offices of inspector general focuses on ideas: a *model* of an "ideal" OIG that is shared among professional networks, which has as its sole goal to contribute to government accountability.

When the Chicago City Council adopted an OIG to conduct oversight over questionable activities of aldermen and their staff, they were responding to the growing norm of independent oversight that I will document in the following pages. But when the Chicago City Council, like so many other elected leaders that I will describe in this book, decided that they weren't so sure that this OIG should have too much power to look into their papers and communications, they withdrew key powers of investigation and independence. And when, after creation of the office, the new OIG nonetheless fought vigorously to carry out real investigations with real teeth, he provided graphic evidence of how much the norm of independent accountability inspires fervent commitment even when institutional mechanisms do not live up to the ideal. Unfortunately, today, the legislative OIG assigned to monitor the Chicago City Council no longer exists, having been done away with in 2015. Nevertheless, this Chicago example is emblematic of the power of the OIG idea—and the efforts by those in political power to have it both ways: to try to enjoy the legitimacy lent by this institutional norm but to also limit its independent power. The tension between these competing impulses is explored in the following pages.

2. Phase I: Conceptualization

Why are offices of inspector general (OIGs) spreading so rapidly among states and localities—or *some* states and localities? To answer this question, it is important to understand the conditions that lead to the adoption of an OIG. We might ask:

- Are jurisdictions adopting OIGs in order to respond functionally to problems of corruption?
- As neoinstitutional theory would suggest, is the adoption of OIGs driven less by particular needs than by the power of normative ideas about accountability?
- Are jurisdictions adopting OIGs as a tool of partisan battle to heighten oversight over political opponents?
- Are OIGs, like any other government agency, simply an expression of a jurisdiction's commitment to the adoption of administrative solutions to problems?
- In adopting OIGs, have jurisdictions learned from each other and, if so, to what extent?

The first phase of adopting an OIG, examined in this chapter, is what I call the conceptualization phase. This is when the concept—the broad idea of adopting an OIG—is: 1) introduced into the jurisdiction, and 2) the idea is endorsed through adoption. During this phase, demands for accountability result in proposals to adopt OIGs. I theorize that OIGs have come to be perceived as a legitimate approach to provide government accountability and a method to meet normative desires for increased oversight of bureaucratic agencies. Specifically, I posit that theories of neo-institutionalism provide a better explanation for the spread of OIGs than alternative explanations.

First, I turn to survey and interview data to demonstrate how the theories of neoinstitutionalism and agenda setting, coupled with the norm of accountability, best explain the conceptualization phase of OIG adoption. To understand the data, John W. Kingdon's theory of policy streams as a basis of policy agenda setting is employed as a framework,[1] demonstrating that OIGs gain a place on the policy agenda as a normative solution to broadly defined government accountability deficits. Second, using an event history analysis (EHA), which has often been used to examine the conditions that influence the diffusion of policies, I test and reject the hypotheses that OIG adoptions represent responses to long-term corruption, growth in administrative bureaucracy, or partisan dominance (or competition). I also reject other explanations relating to theories of policy diffusion and learning by examining the influence of neighboring jurisdictions and the increasing number of OIGs on the federal level or state-level of OIG adoption.

AGENDA SETTING AND THE POWER OF THE OIG IDEA: THE CONCEPTUALIZATION AND ADOPTION OF OIGS

A policy agenda is "the list of subjects or problems to which government officials, and people outside the government closely associated with those officials, are paying some serious attention at any time."[2] Due to time limitations, policymakers can only pay attention to so many problems at one time. Building on James G. March, and Johan P. Olsen's "garbage can" model of the policy process,[3] Kingdon suggests that for any problem to receive attention, three "streams" of thought must come together simultaneously for an item to move up on the policy agenda.[4] These are the problem stream, the policy stream, and the political stream. The problem stream is made up of various pieces of information about a vague policy problem, which often coheres into a clear definition upon the advent of a focusing event or crisis. The policy stream includes the various solutions that could be applied to the problem. This stream unifies into a single solution that becomes preferred over others. Finally, the political stream refers to the political climate, which can be either amenable to political action or indisposed to pursue a solution to the problem. Kingdon suggests that if key stakeholders agree on a problem definition and a policy solution at a time when the political climate is ready for the adoption of the solution, an issue will move onto the policy agenda and be acted on, often with the push of a policy entrepreneur.[5] In the case of OIGs, the power of neoinstitutional norms of accountability and the OIG model are evident in each of these streams.

Offices of Inspector General and Problem Definition

Why are OIGs introduced as a proposed solution for a problem? What is the primary purpose for these proposed OIGs? How does Kingdon's problem stream converge into a single problem for which the OIG is the solution? My survey and interview data suggest that government accountability, writ large, is the problem that an OIG was adopted to address. Thus, the "problem" to which OIGs become the solution is a perceived lack of accountability for government agencies, specifically a concern about waste, fraud, and abuse resulting from what is perceived as too little accountability. That said, a deficit of government accountability can encompass a number of specific problems related to government performance and spending. The data show that OIGs are adopted to address a variety of specific problems under the broad heading of *accountability*. These specific performance and spending problems are not new to government, but rather, what is new is identifying performance and corruption issues as *accountability* issues.

Respondents to my survey commonly identified the reduction of fraud, waste, and abuse as the primary goal for the adoption of an OIG. A full 64 percent of all survey respondents state that this was the *primary goal* of establishing their OIG, and 32 percent state that fraud, waste, and abuse held a *lot of importance* in the establishment of their OIGs. Other common goals, such as improving the effectiveness and the efficiency of government programs, were cited as the primary goal by only 28 percent and 19 percent of all respondents respectively. Responses from state-level OIGs and local/multijurisdictional OIGs did not vary to a great extent, except that issues of program effectiveness and efficiency were of less importance to the establishment of local and multijurisdictional OIGs than issues of fraud, waste, and abuse. These survey responses are summarized in table 2.1.

Several survey respondents commented on other reasons that led to the creation of their OIGs. Comments include: to address liability issues, to improve integrity, to lower child mortality, to provide accountability, to support ethical practices, to provide support to executive management and supervisors, to improve compliance with federal oversight, to address concerns about contracting and procurement, and to lend a level of objectivity to investigations.

An additional reason for an OIG is found in legislative testimony from Connecticut in favor of a statutory OIG. One legislator stated:

> We need an inspector general. I am convinced that this office will help restore the public's confidence in State government and will ensure that we have adequate safeguards against the loss of State assets. This is what this office is all about, and clearly, ladies and gentlemen, for those of you who have been here for a few years, you well know that there has been much money lost in mismanagement in state government.[6]

The common thread of all these concerns is a sense that an OIG can solve a plethora of problems by finding fraud, improving government programs

Table 2.1. Survey Question: How Important Were the Following Goals to the Establishment of Your OIG?

	Was the primary goal	A lot	Some/ a little	Not at all	Total responses
Answer: To reduce fraud, waste, and abuse					
All OIG respondents	33 (63%)	17 (33%)	2 (4%)	0 (0%)	52
State OIGs	22 (61%)	12 (33%)	2 (6%)	0 (0%)	36
Local/Multijurisdictional OIGs	11 (69%)	5 (31%)	0 (0%)	0 (0%)	16
Answer: To improve the effectiveness of government programs					
All OIG respondents	13 (28%)	28 (61%)	4 (9%)	1 (2%)	48
State OIGs	11 (33%)	21 (64%)	1 (3%)	0 (0%)	33
Local/Multijurisdictional OIGs	2 (13%)	9 (60%)	3 (20%)	1 (7%)	15
Answer: To improve the efficiency (reduce costs) of government programs					
All OIG respondents	9 (18%)	31 (64%)	9 (18%)	0 (0%)	49
State OIGs	7 (21%)	20 (58%)	7 (21%)	0 (0%)	34
Local/Multijurisdictional OIGs	2 (13%)	11 (74%)	2 (13%)	0 (0%)	15
Answer: Other					
All OIG respondents	2	1	1	3	7
State OIGs	2	1	1	2	6
Local/Multijurisdictional OIGs	0	0	0	1	1

and operations, and providing public confidence in government. In short, for supporters of OIGs, they are a solution to a range of problems that all relate to government performance and accountability.[7]

A generalized concern about government performance is frequently augmented by a focusing event, such as concern about a highly publicized case of fraud, waste, and/or abuse occurring in the jurisdiction.[8] Nearly half (46 percent) of all survey respondents pointed to a government corruption scandal or scandals as having a primary influence on the establishment of their OIG, although for local and multijurisdictional OIGs, a scandal is more frequently reported as a primary influence compared to state-level OIGs. In addition, 32 percent of all respondents say such scandals had either a lot, some, or a little influence in their jurisdiction toward the establishment of their OIG. On the other end of the scale, only 20 percent of all respondents (and 0 percent of local/multijurisdictional respondents) note that a corruption scandal had no influence on the establishment of their OIG. These results of this survey question are found in table 2.2 as follows.

Narratives about the creation of OIGs provide detail about such focusing events. I asked the interviewees to tell me the story behind the creation of their

Table 2.2. Survey Question: How Much Did a Government Corruption Scandal or Scandals Influence the Establishment of Your OIG?

Respondents	Was the primary influence	A lot	Some/ a little	Not at all	Total responses
All OIGs	19 (46%)	7 (17%)	7 (17%)	8 (20%)	41
State OIGs	11 (37%)	5 (17%)	6 (20%)	8 (26%)	30
Local/multijurisdictional OIGs	8 (73%)	2 (18%)	1 (9%)	0 (0%)	11

OIG. The interviews coupled with news reports at the time demonstrate that following a big public corruption scandal, these OIGs were proposed as the appropriate response.[9]

An example of a focusing event leading to the proposal of an OIG to solve the problem is found in Massachusetts. Massachusetts is the home of the first statewide OIG,[10] which was established by the legislature, the Massachusetts General Court, by statute in 1980.[11] The OIG was born out of work directly related to widespread allegations of corruption in public construction contracting.[12] It was proposed as an essential component of a larger package of statutory reforms.

The history of the formation of the Massachusetts OIG is well documented. Following reports of pieces of buildings on the University of Massachusetts Boston campus dropping and risking injury to the public and the convictions of two state senators on charges of extortion, the General Court created a special commission to investigate corruption related to public construction and to propose legislation to address the problems.[13] This commission became known as the Ward Commission, named after the chair John William Ward,[14] an American history professor and former president of Amherst College.[15] It was made up of reputable citizens, including the Massachusetts attorney general, a professor from the Suffolk University School of Management, an architect, two attorneys from prominent Boston law firms, and a professor of civil engineering at Southeastern Massachusetts University, who met for nearly three years and drafted a twelve-volume report of their findings and recommendations.[16]

The Ward Commission's final report provides an extensive review of how the award of public construction contracts had become intertwined with political donations, kickbacks, political favors, and bribes. Through a careful review of testimony and documents, the commission noted that both political parties were implicated in this culture of corruption.[17] The Ward Commission concluded:

In the award of design contracts for the construction of state and county buildings, we have learned that—

- Corruption is a way of life in the Commonwealth of Massachusetts
- Political influence, not professional performance, is the prime criterion in doing business with the state
- Shoddy work and debased standards are the norm
- The "system" of administration is inchoate and inferior.[18]

The Commission suggested a number of legislative reforms to address the problems, including the creation of an agency to oversee public buildings and public construction; improved regulation of public construction; the establishment of an ethics commission; several components of campaign finance reform; increased criminal penalties for bribery, extortion and false record keeping; and the adoption of an OIG.[19] The OIG was touted as an important tool because the Commission concluded that the Commonwealth lacked the capacity to be "self-critical" and "self-corrective."[20] Hearing testimony from a federal inspector general, the Commission concluded that although the attorney general could address specific cases of allegations of fraud on a case-by-case basis, and the state auditor could review state transactions, neither could complete investigations into systemic fraud or abuse.[21] The OIG was proposed to not only investigate fraudulent and abusive practices but to reduce program costs diverted to corruption, correct wasteful practices, and support prosecution of fraud and corruption.[22]

Illinois offers a similar case, where a focusing event was the occasion for consideration of an OIG. As in Massachusetts, the OIG for the Illinois Department of Children and Family Services was created directly in response to a public scandal, but in Illinois the scandal was a real tragedy: the murder of a child by his mother, Amanda Wallace, both of whom had been under the care of the Department of Children and Family Services.[23] Wallace had been a ward of the state since the age of seven.[24] She had been in and out of foster homes and mental institutions due to violent and criminal behavior toward herself and others. According to the *Chicago Tribune*, "From 1987 until 1992, Elgin [a suburb of Chicago] police compiled 68 reports involving Wallace."[25] During this period of time, Wallace conceived a son with a fellow mental hospital resident.[26] Although the child was immediately taken into foster care upon his birth, Wallace petitioned to be reunited with her son, and, in fact, the child was returned to her and removed from her two times, before the final, fatal time.[27] In 1993, with an even younger son in the bedroom nearby, Wallace hung her three-year-old son.[28]

After his death, the public was so outraged about the fact that this woman and her child had so clearly slipped through the cracks that they demanded a solution through letters to the editor immediately following the tragedy and for several years after the event.[29] Several newspapers added to the pressure with editorials.[30] For example, the *Chicago Tribune* stated: "The child welfare and juvenile justice systems cannot go on as they have, jolted briefly, but not significantly, by each tragic murder of a child."[31] The governor at the time, Jim Edgar, reportedly proposed the OIG to "weed out bad managers and caseworkers" in the Department of Children and Family Services.[32] He proposed an OIG along with other legislative reforms to address the standards that family court judges use when considering cases of family reunification.[33]

These data show that although perceptions of the problem to be addressed vary from jurisdiction to jurisdiction, the common pattern overall is a perception that government or a specific agency has lost its ability to perform as desired for the public good. Poor performance coupled with lax oversight unifies within the problem stream and becomes a government accountability problem for which a solution is needed.[34] This failure to meet the norm of accountability becomes a rallying cry for a solution.

Offices of Inspector General as Policy Solutions

In each of these jurisdictions, many other solutions might have been proposed to deal with these various accountability problems. Elected officials might have called for prosecution; they might have demanded that an agency head institute reforms; they might have even taken on the task themselves and devised a specific statutory reform of an agency or program. Instead, in all these jurisdictions they identified an OIG as the appropriate solution. As neoinstitutional theories would suggest, the idea of an OIG has become a powerful normative model for how to address the perceived problem of lack of accountability. Indeed, OIGs are widely endorsed as *the* key bureaucratic accountability mechanism.

In state after state, the OIG concept has been proposed by a policy entrepreneur. My survey of state and local OIGs indicates that political policy leaders, such as legislators, executive leaders, and agency heads, are the primary individuals who bring the OIG concept to their jurisdictions (see table 2.3). This includes 32 percent of all respondents noting that a legislator or legislators came up with the idea of establishing an OIG and 23 percent pointing to executive heads (i.e., the governor or mayor) as the source of the idea. The next most prominent source (21 percent) is the head of the agency/agencies to be overseen (i.e., high-level government appointees).[35] Occasionally career accountability bureaucrats are identified as the source of idea.

Table 2.3. Survey Question: Who Came Up with the Idea of Establishing Your OIG? (Please Select All That Apply): Answers from All Respondent OIGs

	Responses	%
A legislator or legislators	14	32
The head of the executive branch, such as the governor or mayor	10	23
The head of the agency/agencies to be overseen	9	21
Interest groups or citizen advocates	3	7
An individual running for political office	1	2
Lawyers in public service (not prosecutors)	1	2
Local, state, or federal prosecutors	1	2
The media	0	0
Lawyers in private practice	0	0
Other individual or entity	5	11

Total responses: 44

The survey also indicates that, unlike the diffusion of the Amber Alert or stiffer penalties for drunk driving,[36] there is no clamoring for an OIG by advocacy groups or the media. This latter finding is quite different than typical findings in diffusion studies, that interest groups have a large role in both the diffusion process.[37] In short, the agents of the phenomenon of the diffusion of OIGs are found within the government itself, either elected or appointed. tables 2.4 and 2.5 break out responses from state OIGs and local/multijurisdic-

Table 2.4. Survey Question: Who Came Up with the Idea of Establishing Your OIG? (Please Select All That Apply): Answers from State OIGs Only

	Responses	%
A legislator or legislators	9	28
The head of the executive branch, such as the governor or mayor	9	28
The head of the agency/agencies to be overseen	6	19
Interest groups or citizen advocates	1	3
An individual running for political office	0	0
Lawyers in public service (not prosecutors)	1	3
The media	0	0
Local, state, or federal prosecutors	0	0
Lawyers in private practice	0	0
Other individual or entity	6	19

Table 2.5. Survey Question: Who Came Up with the Idea of Establishing Your OIG? (Please Select All That Apply): Answers from Local/ Multijurisdictional OIGs Only

	Responses	%
A legislator or legislators	5	38
The head of the executive branch, such as the governor or mayor	3	23
The head of the agency/agencies to be overseen	2	15
Interest groups or citizen advocates	2	15
An individual running for political office	1	8
Lawyers in public service (not prosecutors)	0	0
Local, state, or federal prosecutors	0	0
The media	0	0
Lawyers in private practice	0	0
Other individual or entity	0	0

tion OIGs for comparison. These tables show remarkably similar results from both sets of respondents.

Four of five respondents who reported that the survey categories did not include the policy entrepreneur that introduced the idea of an OIG in their jurisdiction, each of whom represented state-level OIGs, pointed to leaders in existing oversight units as the source of the idea. The fifth identified a federal judge.

The positive normative value of an OIG as a policy solution seems especially prominent in two contexts:

- Within widespread patterns of corruption and recent scandals, a candidate for elected office tries to distinguish themself from the corruption by campaigning to launch a new era of good government. In the process, they promise to enact an OIG as a symbol of this commitment.[38]
- Public sector professionals within the jurisdiction propose the adoption of an OIG as a method to improve accountability as a measure of "good government."[39]

Examples of both these cases follow.

The OIG for the Minnesota Department of Human Services was promoted as part of a gubernatorial campaign. The candidate for governor at the time, Mark Dayton, ran on a platform of increased government accountability.[40] The governor's newly appointed commissioner for the Department of Human

Services seized on the OIG concept as a method to support the Governor's priorities, pointing to the health and human services OIGs on the federal level and in other states as inspiration.[41] The press release announcing the new office emphasized: "This change is part of an increased emphasis by DHS on fraud prevention and recovery, furthering Gov. Mark Dayton's commitment toward cultivating a more transparent state government that works for all Minnesotans."[42]

Likewise, the catalyst for OIGs in Florida and Indiana were newly elected governors, both of whom had worked with the federal government and had become familiar with the federal OIG system. Florida's governor Lawton Chiles had served in the US Senate during the time that the IG Act of 1978 and its 1988 amendment were enacted.[43] After his election, he introduced a bill that placed OIGs in every state agency.[44] Similarly, Governor Mitch Daniels of Indiana entered elected office directly after serving as the director of the US Office of Management and Budget under President George W. Bush.[45] Upon his election as governor, Daniels immediately created a statewide ethics OIG by executive order, which was endorsed by the Indiana General Assembly in the proceeding legislative session.[46]

In Illinois, a state beset with a long-term culture of corruption, two OIGs were adopted upon the simultaneous exposure of a major public scandal and the election of a candidate who proposed an OIG as part of a political platform. The first example is the creation of an OIG for the city of Chicago. Mayor Richard M. Daley, the son of Mayor Richard J. Daley, made a campaign promise to create an OIG.[47] Daley used this OIG campaign promise to distinguish himself from the sitting mayor, Eugene Sawyer, a popular politician who had admitted a failure in filing taxes. Daley also wanted to establish himself as standing on ethical high ground, perhaps in part because several of his staff were accused of forging petition signatures.[48] He also used it to distance himself from his father, the well-known, powerful political boss who had been tainted by scandal.[49] The OIG for the city of Chicago was created in 1989 less than one year after Mayor Daley's election.[50]

In 2002–2003, Illinois governor Rod Blagojevich ran on the issue of ethics reform. His plan included ending "pay-to-play" contracting and government corruption.[51] The candidate took this position as the corruption scandal related to his predecessor, Governor George Ryan, emerged.[52] Governor Ryan was eventually indicted and convicted, along with several of his aides, for using his campaign organization and his previous position as secretary of state to promote his political aims.[53] Federal prosecutors documented multiple instances of the misuse of the granting of state contracts and licenses. Soon after being elected, Governor Blagojevich established an executive branch OIG by executive order to oversee the agencies under the governor's jurisdiction[54] and pushed through legislation to codify a set of OIGs in each of the constitutional offices within one year of his election.[55] Governor Blagojevich chose to pursue the creation of an OIG, and held the OIG up as a solution to the ethical problems in the state, despite the fact that Governor Ryan's own inspector general had become implicated in Ryan's corruption schemes and ultimately pleaded guilty to obstructing justice.[56] Although this might suggest that an OIG in Illinois amounts to empty symbolism, the OIG and ethics system that Blagojevich endorsed created a system of OIG monitoring, ethics training, and sanctions for state employees that had not existed before, and which remains alive and well.

An example of an OIG proposed by professional public administrators can be found in the Colorado Department of Corrections. Initially, the department's executive director created the unit as an internal affairs unit to provide an investigative presence in the department, staffed by correctional experts.[57] The department's leadership believed that this unit would be more responsive to major crimes, such as homicides, within correction facilities than external law enforcement because internal staff would better understand the closed culture of a prison.[58] Further, there were concerns that traditional supervision of staff misconduct had become inadequate with the increase in size of the correction system.[59] The Department of Corrections requested that the General Assembly (the Colorado legislature) codify the role in statute, mainly to assure the legitimacy of granting the OIG staff the authority to carry guns and serve as law enforcement officers.[60] Another reason for the legislation, according to legislative staff summaries at the time, was to authorize a small reorganization of the unit.[61] The existing investigative staff were located in the executive director's office and reported to the deputy director.[62] The legislation created the position of IG, who would oversee the OIG and report to the executive director.[63]

Another example of an OIG promoted by professional staff is found in the city of Richmond, Virginia. The city auditor of Richmond had identified instances of fraud in the course of his work, but he felt that sufficiently looking into those issues would be outside his jurisdiction and expertise.[64] He approached the city council about creating an OIG to investigate fraud, and the council agreed,[65] creating a new OIG in ordinance.[66] A nearly identical story is found in Pinellas County, Florida, where the OIG was initiated by internal audit staff[67] and adopted by the county clerk of the court and comptroller.[68]

All these examples demonstrate how the OIG has become the dominant policy solution to the broad problem of accountability. In each case the desire to pursue the norm of accountability pushes the OIG to the forefront of many other possible solutions in the policy stream.[69] Thus, OIGs have become a key bureaucratic expression of the norm of accountability.

Table 2.6. Survey Question: Which of the Following Best Describes the Legal Form of the Establishment of Your OIG? Answers from All OIG Respondents

	Responses	%
The OIG was established in legislation by the legislative body of your jurisdiction, such as the state legislature or city council	36	61
The OIG was established under an agency head's discretion	10	17
The OIG was established by written executive order	8	14
The OIG was established under the executive leader's discretion, but not by written executive order	3	5
Other	2	3
Total	59	100

Total responses: 59

Offices of Inspector General and Political Climate

As Kingdon suggests, a final condition is necessary for adoption of a key policy proposal: the political climate must become favorable to the solution proposed in the policy stream.[70] The current political climate is very much in favor of addressing accountability problems.[71] As one of my interviewees stated: "It is hard to be opposed to accountability."[72]

Political support for the OIG concept is necessary even when a policy is adopted by means other than legislation, as is the case with many OIGs. In fact, nearly 40 percent of OIGs were adopted in other ways. As table 2.6 shows, 22 percent of all survey respondents noted their OIG was formed purely under the discretion of the agency head or the head of the executive branch, and 14 percent were established more formally, albeit still through the use of executive discretion, by executive order. Tables 2.7 and 2.8 break down responses from state OIGs and local/multijurisdiction OIGs for comparison. These tables show that local OIGs, in comparison to state OIGs, are frequently created formally in statute.

Other means of establishment noted by respondents when responding to the follow-up question include being established by federal court order and later codified in statute, and established by voters with the passage of a new city charter. The former answer was offered by a state OIG, while the second was offered by a local OIG.

One might imagine that political climate is a more important factor when considering the adoption of an OIG by legislative action rather than by a discre-

Table 2.7. Survey Question: Which of the Following Best Describes the Legal Form of the Establishment of Your OIG? Answers from State OIGs Only

	Responses	%
The OIG was established in legislation by the legislative body of your jurisdiction, such as the state legislature or city council	22	57
The OIG was established under an agency head's discretion	9	23
The OIG was established by written executive order	6	15
The OIG was established under the executive leader's discretion, but not by written executive order	2	5
Other	0	0
Total	39	100

tionary act; however, political actors, whether elected or appointed, are unlikely to adopt an OIG unless the OIG is politically attractive. The key difference is that governors or agency heads need not encounter political delays. They can create OIGs immediately and then claim credit for the solution to the accountability problem.

For those OIGs that are adopted through formal legislative action, the process is not always immediate. Scholars have noted that policy innovations often take considerable time between initial proposal and final adoption,[73] and this is true with legislatively created OIGs as well. The idea is often introduced over a period of years before being adopted. Although a protracted process

Table 2.8. Survey Question: Which of the Following Best Describes the Legal Form of the Establishment of Your OIG? Answers from Local/ Multijurisdictional OIGs Only

	Responses	%
The OIG was established in legislation by the legislative body of your jurisdiction, such as the state legislature or city council	14	70
The OIG was established under an agency head's discretion	1	5
The OIG was established by written executive order	2	10
The OIG was established under the executive leader's discretion, but not by written executive order	1	5
Other	2	10
Total	20	100

was not the rule in many of the jurisdictions I examined, there are several examples in my case studies where multiple years passed from initial introduction to formal adoption.

One example is found in Cook County, Illinois. In 1988, newspapers reported that the county board president was considering backing off on his campaign promise to create a county OIG.[74] He had argued for the creation of an OIG following an incident wherein county employees were found stealing paint, lumber, and other similar materials; however, after election, he stated that he was not sure that another bureaucracy was needed.[75] The OIG was eventually created eleven years later in 2004,[76] but it was formalized as an independent office in ordinance in 2006.[77]

Likewise, a bill to create an OIG for the Illinois Tollway was first introduced in the Illinois General Assembly in 1994, but it did not go anywhere.[78] Following the indictment of the Tollway director in 1997 for stealing $250,000 and other fraudulent practices, a second bill was introduced. It was opposed both by a citizen's watchdog group, who argued the bill did not create an OIG with enough teeth, and Tollway staff, who argued that problems had been corrected and that they were already audited by the state's auditor general.[79] A third bill was introduced in 2002 after the Tollway was roundly criticized for building a new headquarters, dubbed the Taj Mahal, for $25 million.[80] This bill ultimately failed because a legislator inserted an amendment that required a certain type of expensive brick to be used for any Tollway sound barriers.[81] Because of this addition, the bill was vetoed. An internal office of investigations was created by the Tollway board, and with the help of a legislator, a bill was finally passed in 2010 to create the Tollway OIG.[82]

A final example is found in Minnesota. In this state, three different legislators had introduced four bills in 2008 and 2010 to create an OIG for the Minnesota public health programs, several years prior to the commissioner's creation of an OIG for the Department of Human Services.[83] The bills did not pass; however, after the commissioner announced the creation of the agency's OIG in 2011, these legislators claimed credit for the idea.[84] To date, the Minnesota legislature has passed a statutory reference to the OIG, which assigns it duties related to fraud investigations, but a more formal adoption has yet to be considered.[85]

Although the process to get an OIG on the legislative or policy making agenda may be protracted, typically there is little opposition to an OIG when it is adopted. Very few survey respondents, whether on the state, local, or multijurisdictional levels, identified opponents. The largest groups identified by all respondents were preexisting oversight agencies and heads of the agency or agencies to be overseen, as is illustrated in table 2.9.

Interviewees' comments further illustrate these patterns. Most interviewees

Table 2.9. Survey Question: After the Concept of an OIG Was Introduced, to What Degree Did the Following Individuals or Organizations Support or Oppose the Establishment of Your OIG?

	Strongly supported or somewhat supported (%)	Neutral (%)	Strongly opposed or somewhat opposed (%)	Total responses
Answer: Interest groups or citizen advocates				
All OIG respondents	26 (87)	3 (10)	1 (3)	30
State OIGs	15 (83)	2 (11)	1 (6)	18
Local/multijurisdictional OIGs	11 (92)	1 (8)	0 (0)	12
Answer: Legislators				
All OIG respondents	28 (85)	4 (12)	1 (3)	33
State OIGs	19 (90)	1 (5)	1 (5)	21
Local/multijurisdictional OIGs	9 (75)	3 (25)	0 (0)	12
Answer: The media				
All OIG respondents	23 (82)	5 (1)	0 (0)	28
State OIGs	12 (80)	3 (20)	0 (0)	15
Local/multijurisdictional OIGs	11 (85)	2 (15)	0 (0)	13
Answer: The head of the executive branch, such as the governor or mayor				
All OIG respondents	32 (80)	5 (13)	3 (7)	40
State OIGs	24 (89)	3 (11)	0 (0)	27
Local/multijurisdictional OIGs	8 (62)	2 (1)	3 (23)	13
Answer: The public at large				
All OIG respondents	20 (77)	6 (23)	0 (0)	26
State OIGs	11 (79)	3 (21)	0 (0)	14
Local/multijurisdictional OIGs	9 (75)	3 (25)	0 (0)	12
Answer: The head of the agency/agencies to be overseen				
All OIG respondents	26 (68)	8 (21)	4 (11)	38
State OIGs	23 (85)	3 (11)	1 (4)	27
Local/multijurisdictional OIGs	3 (27)	5 (4)	3 (27)	11
Answer: Local, state, or federal prosecutors				
All OIG respondents	19 ()	7 ()	1 (4)	27
State OIGs	15 (75)	4 (20)	1 (5)	20
Local/multijurisdictional OIGs	4 (57)	3 (43)	0 (0)	7
Answer: Lawyers in public service (not prosecutors)				
All OIG respondents	11 (69)	4 (25)	1 (6)	16
State OIGs	9 (82)	2 (18)	0 (0)	11
Local/multijurisdictional OIGs	2 (40)	2 (40)	1 (20)	5

(continued on the next page)

Table 2.9. *continued*

	Strongly supported or somewhat supported (%)	Neutral (%)	Strongly opposed or somewhat opposed (%)	Total responses
Answer: Lawyers in private practice				
All OIG respondents	10 (55)	5 (28)	3 (17)	18
State OIGs	8 (66)	2 (17)	2 (17)	12
Local/multijurisdictional OIGs	2 (33)	3 (50)	1 (17)	6
Answer: A preexisting oversight agency				
All OIG respondents	10 (48)	6 (28)	5 (24)	21
State OIGs	9 (56)	4 (25)	3 (19)	16
Local/multijurisdictional OIGs	1 (20)	2 (40)	2 (40)	5
Answer: Other interested individual or entity				
All OIG respondents	2 (25)	6 (75)	0 (0)	8
State OIGs	1 (17)	5 (83)	0 (0)	6
Local/multijurisdictional OIGs	1 (50)	1 (50)	0 (0)	2

stated there was no opposition to the creation of their OIG.[86] The following quotes illustrate this point:

- Regarding the creation of a local OIG: Interviewer: "Were there any opponents to the concept?" Respondent: "No. At that time, there were none."[87]
- Regarding the conversion of a local internal audit unit to an OIG: Interviewer: "When you changed the name of the OIG, was there any opposition?" Respondent: "No."[88]
- Regarding a state agency OIG created by the legislature following a public scandal: "[There were] no opponents. I think everyone was so horrified."[89]
- Regarding a statewide OIG created in statute: "It was almost like a World War I Sarajevo assassination, all that kind of stuff. There were powder kegs that had been found in audits. It was one of the governor's campaign promises, to bring accountability and integrity across the government. ... Obviously [the legislature] saw the writing on the wall and thought it would be a good thing."[90]
- Regarding an internal OIG, created by a state agency head through their discretion: "I would hear from people that [the OIG] was their idea ...

I told the [agency head] that the theme out there is: finally, someone at this agency listened."[91]

- Regarding the passage of a state statute creating several state OIGs: "I don't know of anybody that fiercely fought the bill at all."[92]
- Regarding the creation of a local OIG in ordinance: "I think that it's hard to publicly oppose an inspector general's office, especially in the wake of a scandal. I think you saw a lot of public support and behind the scenes, some grumbling."[93]

When opposition was noted, it was from individuals who did not want to be overseen by the OIG, and, in particular, one whose IG was chosen by someone who could potentially be a political enemy,[94] or unions who wanted to make sure their employees would maintain their union rights.[95] For example, when Governor Blagojevich proposed the creation of an OIG to oversee the whole of the executive branch, the other constitutionally elected officials, the comptroller, the treasurer, the attorney general, and the auditor general argued against the Governor's appointment of someone who would oversee their offices.[96] Nevertheless, at the conceptualization phase, these protests are few and far between.

Absence of opposition is striking in that 66 percent of all survey respondents reported that at the time their OIG was created, there was at least one, and as many as seven, nonfederal entities already overseeing the agency/agencies that were within the proposed OIG's jurisdiction. (To be sure, fewer local and multijurisdictional OIGs reported preexisting oversight.) These survey results follow in table 2.10. The number of reported preexisting oversight entities is shown in figure 2.1.

In summary, the norm of accountability as embodied in an OIG make the OIG a politically attractive policy solution to accountability problems. Even though the OIG may not be adopted automatically in every jurisdiction, the facts that policymakers rarely consider other possible solutions and very few opponents to the OIG step forward, even though other oversight entities may already be in place, illustrates the power of the norm.

ALTERNATIVE EXPLANATIONS

My focus on the power of the OIG idea is somewhat different from standard explanations of policy diffusion, and so it makes sense to consider whether these standard explanations provide a better description of the adoption of OIGs. It is certainly true that adoptions of common policies often follow a

Table 2.10. Survey Question: At the Time the Establishment of Your OIG Was Being Considered, Were There Other Nonfederal Agencies, Such as Internal Auditors, Legislative Auditors, etc., Who Had Oversight for the Same Agency/Agencies the OIG Was Intended to Oversee?

	Response	%
	All respondent OIGs	
Yes	29	67
No	14	33
Total	43	100
	State OIGs	
Yes	21	78
No	6	22
Total	27	100
	Local/multijurisdictional OIGs	
Yes	7	47
No	8	53
Total	15	100

familiar pattern involving mimicry of neighboring jurisdictions and responsiveness to the actual level of the problem in one's own jurisdiction. Typically, scholars model these patterns using an event history analysis (EHA).[97] So, using data gathered for this study from my survey and other sources, I

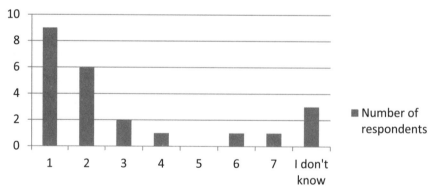

Number of oversight agencies in existence when the OIG was created

Figure 2.1. Bar Chart Showing Number of Preexisting Oversight Agencies Reported by OIG Survey Respondents

conducted an EHA to analyze alternative reasons for the adoption of state-level OIGs.[98]

A benefit of EHA is that it can identify the relationship between the timing of the dependent variable or event, in this case the adoption of an OIG, and covariates of interest, which may also change over time. Additionally, EHA is inherently comparative, because it allows analysis of many observations over time for multiple entities, in this case American states, as opposed to a traditional time series model that utilizes longitudinal data for a single entity.[99] Thus, EHA provides a method by which a researcher can predict the timing of a state's adoption of an OIGs while also factoring in the conditions of those states that have not adopted an OIG during the relevant time period.

My EHA model follows the standard structure for such an analysis. The year of an initial OIG adoption in a state at the state level is a key dependent variable for the EHA. Additional OIG adoptions in the same state are not included in the analysis, even though, as discussed more fully in the second half of this chapter, it is more likely that subsequent OIG adoptions are influenced by previous OIG adoptions in the same state. The adoption variable is coupled with a calculated duration variable, which measures the number of years from 1975, the year the very first state-level OIG was reportedly adopted in Kansas, to the date of adoption, and a censor variable, which indicates with a one or zero whether an OIG was adopted in the state at all. The remaining data used in the analysis are the independent variables, which represent alternative explanations for the diffusion of the OIG concept. Each of these variables is explored in turn below.

Intrastate Conditions of Long-Term Corruption, Size of Bureaucracy, and Partisan Competition

Policy diffusion scholars emphasize that internal conditions in states often influence the adoption of innovations.[100] The internal conditions that affect the rate of adoption relate to both the obstacles of innovation and the impulse to innovate. As Lawrence B. Mohr posited, "the probability of innovation is inversely related to the strength of the obstacles to innovation and directly related to: 1) the motivation to innovate, and 2) the availability of resources for overcoming obstacles."[101] The motivation to innovate and the obstacles against such innovation vary, as the nature of innovation itself varies. As such, the literature on the diffusion of innovations provides a wide range of internal conditions, such as problem severity, state wealth, legislative professionalism, and political ideology, which have been proposed to impact the adoption of an innovation in new locations.[102] This research tests whether several internal conditions of a state either motivate the adoption of an OIG, support over-coming barriers to adoption, or do the opposite: demotivate or erect barriers against the adoption of an OIG. In this EHA, I focus specifically on levels of long-term corruption, size of government, and partisan dominance.

Levels of long-term corruption provide both a strong motivation for a jurisdiction to innovate and adopt an OIG and an obstacle to adopting a unit that provides increased scrutiny. If a state has higher levels of corruption, state policymakers may be greatly interested in adopting additional watchdogs for state government. One would consider this a rational response to a policy problem. Alternatively, high levels of corruption in a state might serve to prevent the creation of an OIG, as powerful actors who are engaged in corrupt practices may oppose establishment of an independent agency with the authority to expose those practices. Similarly, low levels of corruption may indicate a state's commitment to "good government," and this commitment may in turn find expression in widespread support for OIGs as simply another tool to assure good government. To be sure, low levels of corruption might also decrease the perceived need for having an OIG. Thus, while it is plausible that the level of corruption may be related to the adoption of OIGs, it is difficult to predict the direction of the relationship.

Corruption is measured here by the number of federal public corruption convictions in a state, referred to as "convictions." Although it has been shown that there is some bias in conviction data based on the presence of prosecutorial discretion,[103] this is a common measure of relative corruption among the American states. The source of these data is a report from the Department of Political Science and the Institute for Government and Public Affairs of the University of Illinois at Urbana-Champaign, containing convictions in federal court, by federal judicial district, from 1976 through 2010 (the data are compiled from US Department of Justice sources).[104] These scores are summarized and aggregated per state. To normalize the data across states, the totals are divided by 1,000 full-time equivalent (FTE) public employees, state and local, within the borders of the state. The conviction ratio, "convictions," runs from a low of 0.24 (Oregon) to a high of 2 (Louisiana). If higher corruption levels predict an OIG's adoption, states with a higher ratio of convictions per 1,000 FTE public employees should have higher rates of OIG adoption.

Size of government represents a state's investment in its bureaucracy. If adoption of OIGs is an expression of a general state commitment to bureaucracy, we should find that a larger payroll per capita should be positively associated with the adoption of OIGs. Further, a larger, more complicated bureaucracy is at higher risk for inefficiency and ineffectiveness. These factors may provide motivation for adoption of an OIG and, if so, the higher the bureaucratic investment is in a state the higher the rate of OIG adoption should be. This variable, "state investment," is based on states' 2010 annual payrolls (in $1,000s) per 1,000 individuals of the state's population. It runs from a low of $450.51 (Florida) to a high of $1,406.52 (Delaware). A related variable, a legislature's capacity and professionalism, is not included in the model because many state-level OIGs are adopted by actors other than the state legislature, such as governors or agency heads.[105]

Finally, partisan control of the reins of government, or the degree of partisan competition for control of these reins, may influence adoption of OIGs.[106] Some states are solidly controlled by Republicans, others are solidly controlled by Democrats, and in others the party in power may vary between the different branches of government and from election to election. It is possible that the relative level of competition between parties may provide motivation for the creation of an OIG. If a state has a great deal of competition between parties, this will be accompanied with suspicion about how the other party is administering government. This suspicion may provide motivation to adopt an OIG. In a state where one party dominates party government, there may be less motivation to increase bureaucratic oversight. The measure of "partisan competition" (i.e., political control of state government), used here is the Ranney Index.[107] This index weighs popular votes for gubernatorial candidates, the percentage of seats held in state legislatures, and the amount of time a party has held the governorship and the majority of the legislature. Using data dating from 1976 through 2004,[108] I calculated an average score for each state based on the number of observations. The index runs from zero, representing total Republican control, to one, representing total Democrat control, and has a low of 0.272 (Idaho) to a high of 0.792 (Alabama).

I also tested for the influence of other measures of political culture and partisan ideology, including Sharkansky's political culture measure,[109] Putnam's measure of social capital,[110] and several measures developed by R. S. Erikson, G. C. Wright, and J. P. McIver that quantify a state's political ideology and partisan identification of the populace;[111] however, I consistently found these variables had no statistically significant influence on adoption of OIGs. Since these political measures are collinear with partisan competition, as measured by the Ranney Index, I decided, in the name of parsimony, not to include these closely related variables and focus on partisan competition.

The Influence of Other Jurisdictions

In addition to intrastate factors, traditional policy diffusion studies suggest that neighboring jurisdictions learn from each other's experiences, which re-

Table 2.11. Survey Question: How Much Did the Establishment of an OIG in Another Jurisdiction Influence the Establishment of Your OIG?

Respondents	Was the primary influence (%)	A lot (%)	Some/ a little (%)	Not at all (%)	Total responses
All OIGs	2 (6)	3 (8)	13 (36)	19 (50)	37
State OIGs	2 (8)	0 (0)	12 (46)	12 (46)	26
Local/multijurisdictional OIGs	0 (0)	3 (27)	1 (9)	7 (64)	11

duces policy uncertainty.[112] Even though Charles R. Shipan and Craig Volden have suggested that in the contemporary period, with the advent of "low barriers to communication and travel,"[113] the idea of states learning about innovations from their neighbors is simplistic, a map of OIG adoption seems to show that while fairly well-delineated regions of the country have adopted OIGs, other regions have not. Responses to my survey suggest that some state policymakers may have learned from the example of other states—but others report that other states had no influence. As shown in table 2.11, about half of all the respondents to my survey reported that the adoption of an OIG in their jurisdiction was influenced by adoption of OIGs in other jurisdictions, and about half reported that the establishment of an OIG in other jurisdictions had no influence on the creation of their OIG. A higher percentage of respondents from local and multijurisdictional OIGs (64 percent) reported they were not influenced at all by other jurisdictions compared to state OIGs (46 percent).

The follow-up question asked survey respondents to identify the jurisdiction that had an influence on their OIG adoption. The responses suggest that federal OIGs appear to have the greatest influence along with previously existing OIGs within the state. A few other jurisdictions' OIGs are also pointed to by survey respondents, which are listed in table 2.12, but only three other states (Massachusetts, New York, and California) are identified as influential. Only local OIGs pointed to other local OIGs as influential.

These survey results lend some support to learning-based theories of policy diffusion. At the same time, however, the results suggest that, at least in the view of OIG respondents, in many instances neighboring jurisdictions had no influence whatsoever. Since the survey evidence seems mixed, it is unlikely that the adoption of OIGs by neighboring jurisdictions will increase the rates of adoption. Measures of geographical proximity used here were adopted by Frances Stokes Berry and William D. Berry;[114] I calculated the percentage of states sharing a border with the state in question that have previously adopted

Table 2.12. Survey Question: Which Jurisdiction or Jurisdictions Influenced the Establishment of Your OIG?

Federal OIGs:
- Federal OIG system (four respondents)
- US Department of Transportation

State OIGs:
- Massachusetts
- New York
- California Highway Patrol

Previously adopted OIGs in the same jurisdiction:
- Other state agency OIGs in the state (two respondents)
- Various preexisting agencies OIGs in the city of Chicago (two respondents)

Local or other influences:
- New Orleans OIG
- Blue Cross/Blue Shield

an OIG. This measure, "percent neighbors," runs from zero to one. As neither Alaska nor Hawaii have geographical neighbors (nor do they have OIGs), these data are only available for forty-eight states.

On the other hand, of those who do point to other jurisdictions as being an influence (thirteen respondents), five refer to the federal OIG system as influential. Andrew Karch suggests that the dominant influence of federal intervention appears during the agenda setting stage on the state level,[115] and Graeme Boushey notes that federal actions influence the adoption of innovations.[116] With regards to OIG adoption, the federal government does not influence states with typical carrots and sticks, grants and sanctions that are used in such policy areas, such as the federal welfare reform under President Clinton, and which have impacted state policymaking.[117] No federal policy directly encourages states and localities to adopt OIGs. Still, the federal OIG model is prominent and well known and may serve as an informal model for state and local adoption of similar agencies. The model tests for the possible influence of federal OIG adoptions. The measure of federal OIGs is the number of federal OIGs adopted at the time that the state adopted its first OIG.

Analysis and Findings

Using the five variables above, I created the following model:

Rate of OIG adoption
   = f(convictions, state investment, partisan competition, percent of
        neighbors, federal OIGs)

To perform the EHA, I used a Cox Proportional Hazards model, which is a statistical approach that neither requires parametric statistics nor a normal distribution of time to event (i.e., the number of years until the adoption of an OIG in a state). The model is also amenable to discrete periods of time, as is used here, each year being the period of time in question. The Cox model results in the following statistics, rounded to the nearest 0.001, found in table 2.13. A discussion of this model's diagnostics is found in appendix D.

This table shows that three variables have a statistically significant influence on adoption of state OIGS: corruption convictions ($p < 0.05$); adoption by neighbors ($p < 0.05$); and adoption of federal OIGs ($p < 0.01$). However, the latter two variables are in an unexpected direction. Neither the partisan competition variable (Ranney Index) nor the variable reflecting a state's investment in its bureaucracy are statistically significant. The statistically significant findings and accompanying hazard ratios above can be interpreted as follows:

- As the total number of public corruption convictions in a state *increases* by one conviction per 1,000 state FTE, and all other variables are constant, the rate of OIG adoption *decreases* a moderate amount, by 30.2 percent ($1.0 - 0.698 = 0.302$).
- As the percentage of neighbors with OIGs *increases* one unit, and all other variables are held constant, the rate of adoption *decreases* fairly significantly by 89.2 percent ($1.0 - 0.108 = 0.892$).
- As the number of federal OIGs established prior to a state's adoption of an OIG increases by one, and all other variables are held constant, the rate of OIG adoption *decreases* slightly by 5.3 percent ($1.0 - 0.947 = 0.053$).

Among these associations, the easiest interpretable is the significant negative association between corruption convictions and adoption of state-level OIGs. We see that OIGs are *not* a response to federal public integrity convictions. Rather, it may be that states with lower levels of these convictions are also likely to have less government corruption and a culture that emphasizes good government, and it is possible that this variable is tapping this underlying commitment to good government. Thus, this association is consistent with the expectation that states with cultures of commitment to good government are more likely to adopt OIGs, and states with cultures of corruption are less likely to do so. If so, adoption of an OIG is an expression of this underlying commitment. OIGs are of course but one method of improving government accountability, but this analysis suggests that their adoption is consistent with

Table 2.13. Results of the Cox Proportional Hazard Model

Variable	Variable definition	Hazard ratio	Standard error	p value
Corruption convictions	Total number of public corruption convictions in the state from 1976 to 2010, per 1,000 of FTE state and local employees in 2010	0.698	0.103	0.015*
State investment	Total payroll for 2010 for all state employees divided by 1,000 of state population	0.998	0.001	0.106
Partisan competition	The Ranney Index[a] measuring party dominance, running from zero, representing total Republican control, to one, representing total Democrat control	0.782	1.380	0.889
Percent neighbors	Percentage of neighboring states with OIGs prior to a state's adoption of an OIG	0.108	0.102	0.015*
Federal OIGs	The number of federal OIGs established prior to a state's adoption of an OIG	0.947	0.011	0.000**

[a]Austin Ranney, "Parties in State Politics," *Politics in the American States: A Comparative Analysis* (Boston: Little, Brown, 1971).

*Statistically significant at p < 0.05

**Statistically significant at p < 0.01

the active pursuit of other accountability goals, which is reflected in reduced corruption convictions. It is also possible that in states with higher numbers of public corruption convictions over time, policymakers may see federal prosecutors are a successful method of maintaining government accountability and, therefore, feel that they have no need to create an OIG to do the same; however, this explanation is much less convincing. It often takes years for a federal prosecutor to complete a federal corruption case in the federal courts. As a result, the conclusion of a conviction is quite removed in time from the act of corruption.

In other respects, the results are counterintuitive. Despite an apparent regionalism shown through a visual inspection of a map of the United States, adoption of an OIG by a state's neighbors seems to *decrease* the likelihood that a state will adopt an OIG. As additional surrounding states adopt OIGs, the rate of OIG adoption decreases significantly and substantially by nearly 90 percent. This result is consistent with the survey observation that 50 percent of respondents were not influenced by other jurisdictions when they adopted OIGs; but the negative effect suggests that regarding the issue of government accountability and bureaucratic reorganization, states may actually be negatively influenced by the examples of neighbors.

Further, increasing numbers of OIGs on the federal level have a slight negative effect on the rate of state and local OIG adoption. This finding runs counter to the survey respondents' comments shown in table 2.7 and several other sources,[118] all of which suggest that the federal OIG system has positively, rather than negatively, influenced state adoption of an OIG. Additionally, although 50 percent of survey respondents noted that no other jurisdiction had influence on their adoption of an OIG, the EHA analysis indicates that, like the influence of surrounding states' OIG adoptions, increasing numbers of federal OIGs actually discouraged OIG adoption in the state somewhat.

Finally, neither the size of state government nor partisan competition influences the rate of OIG adoptions. States that invest heavily in their government are not more drawn to OIGs overseeing state bureaucracies than states with smaller governments. Also, OIG adoption is not related to sharp competition between the parties or, conversely, to dominance by one of them.

In light of the counterintuitive nature of the statistical results, it is possible that some key influences on adoption of state OIGs have not been included in the model. One strong possibility may be that the idea of an OIG is transferred by subject matter experts within particular policy fields. As mentioned before, the NCSL website has studies of OIGs, but only in the context of a larger substantive policy area, such as Medicaid.[119] It is likely that governmental professionals in particular fields are sharing the idea of an OIG through associations such as the National Association of Medicaid Directors or the American Correctional Association. Survey data show that nineteen states have adopted an OIG to oversee a health and/or human services agency, and eleven states have adopted an OIG to oversee a corrections agency. These are the most common areas for which OIGs are adopted on the state level. Additional evidence supporting this conjecture about field-specific networks includes a statement from an inspector general for a state corrections department who told me that although he does not network with inspectors general in other fields because he does not find it useful, he does talk with his counterparts in other corrections agencies.[120] Similar evidence is shown in the announcement of the creation of the Minnesota Department of Human Services OIG in which the department cited other OIGs in the field of human services as influential.[121]

In sum, the EHA strongly suggests that standard ways of modeling policy diffusion do not provide a simple and clear explanation for widespread adoption of OIGs. This adoption is not related to a state's level of corruption, the size of its bureaucracy, the extent of partisan competition, or adoption of OIGs by other jurisdictions, including the federal government—at least not in ways we might expect from past studies of diffusion.

We are left, then, with the compelling explanation offered by participants in the process, as revealed by my survey and the documentary evidence compiled for this study: supporters of OIG adoption felt a strong need for greater accountability, and saw no effective alternative other than an OIG. It is the idea of accountability, and the idea of an OIG to carry it out, that propels increasingly widespread adoption of this unique agency.

CONCLUSION

This chapter has examined the process of placing the OIG concept on the political agenda and adopting it. In this process, one thing is abundantly clear: the OIG idea has considerable normative power. This chapter has suggested that this idea holds more explanatory power than other rationales, such as levels of corruption, investment in bureaucracy, and partisan competition. The institutionalization of the OIG and the norm it embodies has more influence on OIG adoption than the adoption of OIGs by neighboring states or by the federal government.

John W. Kingdon's[122] description of the three streams of agenda-setting nicely characterizes the process by which the OIG idea takes hold and gains political support. When the idea is initially introduced to the jurisdiction, it is generally proposed by policy entrepreneurs who are either campaigning for an elected office or by professional bureaucrats pursuing "good government." The idea is often introduced following a public scandal, which serves as a focusing event. Nevertheless, during this phase, the role of the OIG tends to be rhetorically inflated as a solution to all manner of governmental ills, suggesting that OIGs are able to solve all manner of problems and bring about accountability. The claims for OIGs' effectiveness are especially striking in light of the fact that OIGs typically have *no* authority to impose solutions but only may collect information and make recommendations. This observation only punctuates the point that OIGs have become a symbolic solution to the perceived need for bureaucratic accountability. This normative power is reemphasized by the fact that the proposal to establish an OIG has remarkably few opponents. Who can oppose greater accountability of government agencies? Who stands in favor of corruption, fraud, and abuse? At least at the conceptualization phase, the idea of an OIG seems unassailable. It is wrapped in the symbolic legitimacy of accountability itself.

Given the power of the norm of accountability and its influence in the widespread adoption of OIGs, it is striking to remember that OIGs have limited authority in the accountability process. Although their role is to monitor government activities through audits, investigations, and reports, they are billed by their proponents as able to address a range of issues, from fixing problems to providing public confidence in the government. The idea of an OIG becomes much bigger and broader than the actual role of an OIG in the accountability process. The normative expectations of OIGs are large and perhaps unrealistic.

In fact, at this initial adoption phase, OIGs seem to have the cachet of a magic wand, able to solve nearly any accountability problem. This high expectation stands in sharp contrast to the reality of OIGs' limited authority: they can report information but not act on this information. An interviewee, the first IG for his jurisdiction, dramatized this conflict between dream and reality:

> I came here and . . . I was asked one day, "What do you think is going to happen when you're here?" And I said, "nothing." And they said, "What do you mean?" And I said, "Nothing, because you are all so apathetic. Change doesn't come from me. Change is going to come from all of you, members of the public, the citizens, finally, when you get sick of seeing the same old thing happen again and again. Because you could have one hundred IGs here, it's not going to matter. Until your voices are made public and they are loud, there won't be change." So that's really the message that I try to tell anyone is that you could put one hundred of me and one hundred of [another IG]

and 100 of everybody else, it doesn't matter. Until you as citizens decide enough is enough, that's when the real changes come. And that goes not just for [this jurisdiction] but for any jurisdiction anywhere, any business, any jurisdiction.[123]

As the limitations of an OIG to affect accountability appear to be ignored in the conceptualization phase, they are similarly overlooked in the design and implementation phases. Instead the norm of accountability overshadows these limitations, but instead of encouraging OIG adoption as is found in this first phase, the new accountability looms large and gives rise to opposition toward an OIG in the design and implementation phases. These phases and the dynamics that arise are addressed in chapters 3 and 4.

3. Phase II: Design

As was demonstrated in the previous chapter, since 1976, the powerful norm of accountability in the context of bureaucratic agencies has come to be embodied by an office of inspector general (OIG). This office has come to be seen as an appropriate—and perhaps the ideal—solution to the problem of ineffective government programs, bureaucratic waste, and corruption. Political leaders who seek to style themselves as bureaucratic reformers have seized on this model as a symbol of their commitment to reform, and professional bureaucrats have proposed OIGs in order to embrace "good government" ideals. Jurisdictions have adopted OIGs mainly at the instigation of these reformers, often after a specific event of public corruption is exposed. This chapter takes the story of the conceptualization and adoption of OIGs to the next stage: the design phase. I explore how the norm of accountability impacts OIG design, and how these designs vary from state to state.

The design phase refers to the point at which pencil is put to paper, and the details of how the OIG will be structured and what the OIG will do are worked out. Sometimes the design phase occurs through a political process resulting in the passage of legislation imposing new oversight on an agency or agencies.[1] Other times, the design process occurs within an agency and results in a reorganization of staff.[2] As this chapter will show, OIGs vary considerably in their design in ways that matter to the pursuit of accountability.

Most studies of policy diffusion examine only whether a policy is *adopted*; they do not go on to examine whether, or how, common policies that are widely adopted vary in their *design*. Those that do will analyze how common policy types vary in their design in relation to varying conditions among jurisdictions, particularly demographic characteristics of the population as a whole, the relative power of particular constituencies or interest groups, the degree of legislative professionalism, or other factors.[3] These scholars call such variations in policies that arise from location to location "reinvention," although Andrew Karch prefers "customization."[4] These terms suggest progressive *improvements in* or *adaptations of* policies to make them appropriate for local conditions. Often, these changes in policy design are credited as progressive improvements to a policy over time, based on learning from other jurisdictions' experiences about policy implementation.

This chapter builds on these studies but reaches a very particular conclusion about the factors shaping the place-to-place variations in the design of

OIGs. In contrast to the image cast by the idea of reinvention, the thesis of this chapter is that many jurisdictional variations in the design of OIGs are best characterized instead as *deliberate debilitation*: the intentional effort, based on a recognition of the potential power of an OIG structured according to the ideal model, to disable the office in ways that undercut its effectiveness. Put another way, in some places the designers of these agencies seem to want to have it both ways: they want the symbolic legitimacy of adopting an office styled as an "inspector general," but they do not want that office to have too much real power and influence.

This thesis rests on the premise that there is a common normative model of an OIG that is remarkably specific regarding its ideal design. This chapter's analysis is structured in relation to this "ideal model," or archetype, as a baseline and describes how OIGs are consistent with or vary from this archetype.

This chapter focuses first on the characteristics of a shared concept of the "ideal" OIG. Second, it explores how state and local OIGs differ from the archetypal OIG and the reasons for this variation. In doing so, I focus on the following four specific areas of variation: 1) the legal form of the OIG's establishment, 2) the duties that the OIG staff perform, 3) the authority granted the OIG to perform its duties, and 4) the independence granted to the OIG

THE COMMON MODEL OF AN "IDEAL," OR ARCHETYPAL, OIG

Since the adoption of the federal Inspector General Act of 1978 (IG Act), a common model of the structure and powers of an OIG has developed. This common model is codified in three sources: the federal IG Act of 1978 (as amended); the *Principles and Standards for Offices of Inspector General*,[5] also known as the Green Book; and "Model Legislation for the Establishment of Offices of Inspector General," both publications of the Association of Inspectors General.[6] The federal legislation is important to consider because it represents the modern civilian OIG, from whence the general idea of an OIG came. It illustrates several innovations that have developed into the shared understanding of an OIG. Building on the federal prototype, the Association's publications provide an outline of an archetypal OIG that is thought to be best positioned to contribute to the accountability process. The model of the Association of Inspectors General expanded out of the federal model, strengthening the characteristics that exemplify what has become a shared understanding of an OIG. These three sources of the elements of the archetype are reviewed briefly, followed by a more detailed description of the OIG archetype.

The Prototype of the OIG Archetype: The Federal
Inspector General Act of 1978

The initial federal model was established with the passage of the IG Act of 1978. By and large, this federal model has not been altered since its first enactment. To be sure, in 1998, a set of less independent federal OIGs were created for thirty-four small agencies headed by independent regulatory boards, and in 2008, oversight and coordination of all federal OIGs was formalized; however, the OIGs for the large cabinet agencies and agencies headed by presidentially appointed secretaries have not changed in design.

Before the passage of the IG Act, Congress made some forays into experimenting with civilian OIGs. First, Congress created an "Inspector General and Comptroller" in 1959 to oversee the State Department, but its legislation was repealed ten years later. This entity had a unique authority in that it could alter or discontinue programs it disapproved of, rather than simply make nonbinding recommendations; however, the inspector general and comptroller never exercised this authority.[7] This authority was eschewed by Congress with the IG Act, and it has not been endorsed by the Association of Inspectors General.

Second, the secretary of agriculture created a nonstatutory OIG in 1962 following the exposure of the infamous Billie Sol Estes scandal. Estes was a Texas businessman who was found to be involved in "clandestine lease-back arrangements, phony mortgages on nonexistent fertilizer storage tanks, illegal transfers of federal-compensation rights, kickbacks for bankers and bribes for Washington. The scams were so complex that prosecutors eventually had to break them down into fifty state and federal indictments."[8] An OIG was one of twelve reforms recommended for the Department of Agriculture by the House Subcommittee on Technology, Information Policy, Intergovernmental Relations and Procurement Reform[9] after an exhaustive investigation into Estes's actions. Fourteen years later, the secretary did away with the OIG, highlighting the weakness of an oversight body established on a discretionary basis.

Third, two statutory OIGs were created in 1976 and 1997, when Congress created OIGs for the US Department of Health, Education, and Welfare and the Department of Energy, respectively. Finally, the federal model of the office of inspector general was formalized with the passage of the IG Act, which created OIGs for twelve large federal agencies. This act established the broadbrush strokes of a federal OIG model that continues to exist today in seventy-three federal OIGs. The IG Act instituted several innovative characteristics that were not present in federal internal oversight. The characteristics of the OIG prototype found in the IG Act have largely been incorporated in the Association of Inspectors General's Green Book and model legislation.

Codifying the OIG Archetype: The Association of Inspectors General's Green Book and Model Legislation

The Association of Inspectors General is the author of the two documents that together make up today's accepted understanding of an archetypal OIG. This association dates back to 1996, when, according to its website, "approximately thirty inspectors general and professional staff met in Atlanta, Georgia. The group recognized the growing trend of the inspector general concept on the federal, state, local, and international level [*sic*]. The need for an organization to provide leadership in the promotion of integrity efforts in government became evident."[10] The Association's mission is "to foster and promote public accountability and integrity in the general areas of prevention, examination, investigation, audit, detection, elimination and prosecution of fraud, waste and abuse, through policy research and analysis; standardization of practices, policies, conduct and ethics."[11] The Association has not only drafted *Principles and Standards for Offices of Inspector General*, also known as the Green Book, and model OIG legislation, but a constitution and bylaws, a policy manual, and strategic plans. It also provides annual training conferences, and it has developed professional certifications for four types of OIG personnel: an IG, an auditor, an investigator, and an inspector/evaluator.[12] The Association has become a vital professional organization bringing together OIG staff from around the world to discuss how to perform OIG work.

A review of the Association's Green Book and model legislation shows that many key components of these documents grew out of the federal legislation; however, characteristics of the federal OIG model have been strengthened in several instances. These key components have gained wide support among the professional networks around OIGs and are widely regarded as key elements of a structure best positioned to provide objective, reliable analyses.

The Office of Inspector General Archetype

Four elements have come to be accepted by OIG practitioners as keys to a strong OIG archetype. These are: 1) the legal form of the OIG's establishment, 2) the complementary duties of audits and investigations, 3) the authority granted the OIG to perform its duties, and 4) the independence granted to the OIG. Each of these elements is discussed separately below.

The first key characteristic of this model is its establishment of OIGs by *statute*. The legal form of the OIG is important as statutory creation ensures that the OIGs cannot be done away with easily by the entity that is overseen if this entity does not like the OIG's oversight. As Paul C. Light states in reference to the internal OIG created by the secretary of agriculture in 1962, "The problem with having one boss and no statutory base is clear: What the secretary giveth, the secretary can take away. Despite the [Department of Agriculture] IG's enviable record and strong endorsement from GAO, Nixon's secretary of agriculture, Earl Butz, abruptly—some say casually—eliminated the position in 1974, dividing it into the two offices from which it came, audit and investigation."[13] Of course, statutes can be repealed, but the hurdles to do this are great and hard to surmount. On the federal level, it requires sufficient salience to land on the legislative agenda, a majority vote of two houses of Congress, and approval by the president. Thus, a statutory foundation provides more permanence and legitimacy than establishment merely at the fiat of an agency executive.

A statutory basis for authority has been endorsed by the Association of Inspectors General. The Association's Green Book states: "An OIG should be formally created as a legal entity. The [Association of Inspectors General] recommends that the OIG be established by statute or, if necessary, by executive order."[14] This legal form should also "establish the OIG's mandate, authority, and powers; provide for confidentiality of records and proceedings; identify qualifications for the inspector general and staff; protect the office's independence; and provide protection to whistleblowers."[15] In furtherance of these principles, the Association of Inspectors General drafted its model legislation.

As one local IG explained, the fact that his OIG was created in statute helps to give the OIG a basis of authority and legitimacy. As a result, the agency management has to "figure out how to work with his office rather than try to get around it."[16] He stated:

> We're created by state statute. So that is definitely stronger than being created by municipal ordinance or some internal board action that creates an IG office. So to change anything, there needs to be legislation. Not to say that couldn't be done, but that gives us more power. And our subpoena power comes from that statute as well. So that gives us more stability that way. That gives us a little independence, because at the whim of some board, they are not going to change some IG rules or [a] board-created IG.[17]

The opposite is true for OIGs that are not created in statute. A deputy IG explained her view about the precarious position of her office as follows:

> If we never get a legislative base for our existence and this [agency head] goes away, I'd be concerned about our—what kind of authority would you call that? Political presence, or something. Because all the long-standing

division directors and everybody are here as they were before the [agency head arrived]. And she is our champion, and [the IG] is our champion, and without her I'm not certain that we wouldn't lose a lot of force and energy and presence and ability. There are persons and functions within a bureaucracy that raise issues and raise challenges, but the bureaucracy doesn't necessarily respond particularly strongly and . . . we could be relegated down . . . quickly if we lost suddenly both of them [the agency head and the IG] with no coverage of authority and rule. So I don't think we should go bare [without statutory authority] ongoing. Doesn't have to be next year, but the year after that for sure we should establish ourselves.[18]

In short, creation in statute provides a firm authority for an OIG to play an independent part in the accountability process by giving it a presence and a level of legitimacy that is recognized by those being overseen and those who may receive and review the OIG's work product.

The second characteristic of an archetypal OIG is that its duties encompass both auditing and investigations. This characteristic was a federal innovation.[19] Prior to the IG Act, investigations and audit were two disciplines that operated separately in federal agencies. Both functions were identified by Congress as being woefully inadequate after the Billie Sol Estes scandal came to light, particularly because the two units operated in silos and did not communicate.[20] The IG Act merged investigation and audit units in order to address fraudulent behavior alongside inefficient practices. An interviewee who worked in the federal OIG system before moving to a state OIG explained:

When we started making IGs in the federal government, what happened with Billie Sol Estes was the underlay of a lot of the Inspector General Act, especially with Department of Agriculture. In that case, the people who were doing the investigations didn't talk to the people who were doing the audits at the Department of Agriculture. And for that reason, [Estes] would run circles around them both. And so afterwards we said, we can't have that happening.[21]

Despite the arguably practical need to strengthen both units, enhanced accountability was a byproduct. Federal OIGs began to investigate compliance with rules and regulations, which is a reactive, or *post-factum*, approach to oversight, and began to carry out audits with an eye toward improving performance, which is a proactive, or *pre-factum*, approach to oversight.[22] Since the decision to bring these two functions together, this combination has been widely viewed as essential to effective oversight. In fact, Melvin J. Dubnick, and

H. George Frederickson assert that to "break or qualify the link between the two [post-factum and pre-factum dimensions of accountability] . . . is something that is accountability in name only."[23]

The ideal of an OIG performing both audits and investigations has been codified in the Green Book and model legislation. The Association suggests that the archetypal OIG "audit, inspect, evaluate, and investigate the activities, records and individuals affiliated with contracts and procurements undertaken by the government entity and any other official act or function of the government entity."[24] Investigations here include "criminal, civil and administrative investigations."[25] Audits encompass the "economy, efficiency, and effectiveness of the agency's operations and functions."[26] Although additional activities, such as training and issuing public reports, are detailed in the model legislation, the Association of Inspectors General emphasizes that OIGs pursue both audit and investigatory disciplines by providing the following comment: "The intent of this section is to detail the authority that the [Association of Inspectors General] recommends be provided to *every* Inspector General function."[27]

A benefit to having both disciplines in one office was explained to me as follows:

> There's a synergistic value to having auditors and investigators work together. And that's what the theory underlying the Office of the Inspector General is. I never wanted to see it be auditors and investigators—I wanted—I don't want to call them "audigators"—but I want them to have both skills. Because I think both of them use the same skill set, they just apply it a little differently. . . . And auditors make good investigators once they get their dander up; I mean they're really good. And investigators make good auditors once they understand what they're doing.[28]

Although most OIGs do not cross-train their employees for carrying out both tasks, this interviewee saw advantages in having both disciplines present—not only to improve accountability and the OIG's work product, but to manage an OIG's resources efficiently. He stated:

> A lot of auditors want to be auditors—that's the truth. And a lot of investigators don't want to audit. But I think you have to have [both]. We just are not big enough to have that degree of specialty. I think there's a comfort level in doing what you know. Well, there probably is, but at the same time, to be effective, you've got to make every resource you have count and you just can't have one resource dedicated that can't work in the other area.[29]

Management concerns aside, an OIG with both investigators and auditors not only identifies wrongdoers and legal violations but reviews systems for weaknesses to prevent wrongdoing before it happens. Combining both disciplines in one OIG allows the OIG to be more holistic in its oversight and provide a wider base of information for the accountability process.

The third characteristic of an archetypal OIG is that it is granted several types of authority to perform its role. Each of these powers helps an OIG collect information, follow the facts where they lead, and then report its findings and recommendations to others in the accountability process. These authorities are found in both the Green Book and model legislation. The list includes:

- The right to full and unrestricted access to agency records and the records of those involved with the agency under its jurisdiction. The OIG keeps any confidential items as such to the extent to the law.[30]
- Access to the head of any public entity when necessary for purposes related to the work of the OIG.[31]
- The authority to subpoena witnesses, administer oaths or affirmations, take testimony, and compel the production of such records as may be relevant.[32] This authority extends to documents and individuals outside the authority of the public entity.
- Law enforcement authority. Law enforcement authority generally includes authorization to carry a firearm on duty; seek and execute warrants for arrest, search and seizure; and make arrests without a warrant when either witnessing a crime or having reasonable grounds to believe a felony has been committed.[33]

Also, the publications include a provision that requires all public employees to report fraud, waste, corruption, illegal acts, and abuse to the OIG.[34] To encourage this reporting, the OIGs are authorized to keep complainants' identities confidential unless disclosure of their identities is unavoidable in the course of an investigation.[35] These provisions are often referred to as whistleblower protections.

Most of these authorities are found in the federal IG Act, as amended, but several have been expanded in the subsequent publications so as to provide an OIG with the full authority it needs to obtain the information required to fully monitor an agency's programs and operations. For example, federal OIGs may use subpoena power to obtain documents relevant to their inquiries; however, they lack the authority to compel testimony.[36] Additionally, the IG Act provides that OIG investigators may be granted law enforcement authority, but only upon application to the attorney general.[37]

The fourth and most important characteristic of an archetypal OIG, which was an innovation of the IG Act, is independence of an OIG from the agency it oversees. As Light states, "At its most elemental level, the IG Act was an organizational device for unifying two simple functions, audit and investigation, into one unit. However, what made the IG Act much more significant was the decision to protect those new units from administration politics."[38] Independence from the agency that the OIG oversees is crucial because it allows the OIG to be in the best position to provide the most objective, reliable information it can without external influence, which is the essence of the OIG role. The Green Book explains: "The inspector general is responsible for establishing and maintaining independence so that OIG opinions, conclusions, judgments, and recommendations will be impartial and viewed by others as impartial."[39]

In order to be independent, both internal and external "impairments," that is, the Green Book's term for risks to the independence of an OIG, must be examined and addressed. Internal impairments arise from an individual's relationships, preconceived ideas, previous involvement or employment, and biases.[40] Such impairments could hinder the individual from fairly evaluating evidence. OIG staff are counseled to evaluate whether they have personal impairments that might create actual or perceived conflicts of interest, which might impact the outcome of a report's conclusions, and disqualify themselves from the project. If disqualification is not possible, the individual must disclose his or her impairments in the final report.

External impairments are those things external to the office that "can restrict the efforts or interfere with the OIG's ability to form independent and objective opinions and conclusions." Specific examples of external restrictions include such things as "influences that jeopardize continued employment of the inspector general or individual OIG staff for reasons other than competency or the need for OIG services"; "restrictions on funds or other resources dedicated to the OIG, such as timely, independent legal counsel, that could prevent the OIG from performing essential work"; interference in the hiring or firing of OIG staff or the selection and scope of the OIG's work; and interference with OIG access to documents or individuals necessary for OIG work.[41]

Personal impairments are largely a matter for OIG management, but external impairments can be prohibited by design. The Association of Inspectors General's model legislation provides guidance on how to protect an OIG's independence from external impairments. First, the model legislation includes a clear statement of intent: "The intent of this legislation is to create a *wholly independent* office of Inspector General."[42] This statement provides a signpost for not only the OIG and the jurisdiction that it oversees but also to the public, who are ultimately the final stakeholders in government accountability.

Second, certain hiring and firing protections are afforded the IG. The model legislation provides for appointment by either the governor with advice and consent of the senate, the governor alone, the legislature, or a high-ranking government official with a position equal to or higher than an agency head over whom the OIG has jurisdiction.[43] The IG holds a term of office of five years, after which they may be reappointed.[44] Finally, the IG may only be removed for cause.[45] The model legislation addresses personal impairments for the IG as well. It states that the IG is selected based on professional qualifications and without regard to political affiliations, and the IG may not have previously served as a manager within the agency for at least five years before appointment.[46]

Third, the model legislation addresses budgetary independence. It states: "The Office of Inspector General will be funded from the General Fund of the Agency and will receive no less than (X percent) of the General Fund's annual appropriation each year."[47] This method of funding aims to ensure that the OIG will receive a guaranteed level of funding each year, which will be directly proportional to the funds allocated for the agency within the OIG's jurisdiction.[48] This funding scheme also removes the OIG budget from the annual political budgetary process.

Fourth, an OIG's independence is buttressed by giving the IG full authority to manage the OIG without interference. The model legislation, much like the federal statute, states: "The Inspector General shall establish the organization structure appropriate to carrying out the responsibilities and functions of the office. The Inspector General shall have the power to appoint, employ, promote, and remove such assistants, employees, and personnel as deemed necessary for the efficient and effective administration of the office."[49] Further, "[The OIG] is operationally independent from the appointment authority, the legislative branch, and the agency. The appointing authority, legislative body, or agency head shall not prevent, impair, or prohibit the Inspector General from initiating, carrying out, or completing any audit, investigation or review."[50]

Finally, to ensure that the OIG's work product has an independent audience, which is necessary for a government actor to ultimately be held accountable for their actions, the model legislation states: "The Inspector General will report the findings of the Office's work to the head of the investigated/audited agency, to the appropriate elected and appointed leadership and to the public. The Inspector General shall also report criminal investigative matters to the appropriate law enforcement agencies."[51]

Further, if any serious or flagrant issues are uncovered, the IG reports this immediately to the agency head, who is required in turn to report the issue to appropriate representatives of the executive and legislative branches, with any comments that the agency head wants to add.[52] The IG issues an annual report that describes its activities over the previous year to the agency head and any interested oversight bodies.[53] Regarding this annual report, the model legislation states: "Upon issuance, members of the media and the public shall be promptly advised of the issuance of the report. Such reports will be provided to their representatives upon request."[54]

FOLLOWING THE MODEL—AND DEVIATING FROM IT

Some designers of state and local OIGs closely follow the recommended archetype. This illustrates its influence. Many other designers, however, deviate from the recommended model in significant ways. Ironically, this, too, illustrates the model's influence, as designers who choose to deviate clearly often do so in order to undercut the OIG's position in the accountability process in specific, well-planned ways. The deliberate deviation occurs in states that have both high and low levels of corruption and states that have both Democratic and Republican control of state government. Two examples illustrate the breadth of variation found across state and local OIGs: the Massachusetts OIG, in a state that tends to have more Democratic control of state government and that falls in the middle range of average federal public corruption convictions, and the Minnesota Department of Human Services OIG, in a state with governance more balanced between parties as measured by the Ranney Index and with very few corruption convictions.

The Massachusetts OIG is an example of an office that does not deviate much from the archetypal model, even though it predates the codification of the model by the Association of Inspectors General. As we saw in the previous chapter, the Massachusetts OIG was designed by the Ward Commission, a special commission that was tasked to examine corruption in contracting for public building construction in the state of Massachusetts. It recommended the creation of an OIG as part of a larger set of reforms to address the problems it found, and it modeled its legislation after the federal OIGs, having taken testimony from a federal IG.[55] The Massachusetts OIG embodies the archetype OIG in several key ways.

First, the Massachusetts OIG was created by statute, and thus has a strong legal base of authority. This statute was adopted in 1980 by the Massachusetts General Court, which is the name for the Massachusetts legislature.[56]

Second, like the archetype, the Massachusetts OIG performs both audits and investigations into fraud, waste, abuse, effectiveness, and efficiency. It can also make recommendations to agencies that arise from its oversight work and weigh in on proposed legislation in relationship to public integrity issues.[57] In addition to these primary oversight activities focused on detecting fraud, the Massachusetts OIG developed an extensive training program based on its mandate to prevent fraud.[58] The OIG administers the Massachusetts Certified Public Purchasing Official (MCPPO) program, which trains public administrators across the state about cost-effective, ethical purchasing practices.[59] In connection with MCPPO training, the OIG created six different certifications, which people can receive through initial training and maintain through continued education. The OIG provides specific assistance on local procurement of supplies, services, equipment, and real property, as well as dispositions of the same, the support of which includes maintaining a hotline for questions from local governmental bodies.[60] Last but not least, it performs statutorily required monitoring of special initiatives, such as Medicaid and large construction projects (e.g., the Big Dig).[61]

Similar to the archetypal OIG, this OIG has several statutory provisions that provide it legal authority to pursue its mission. For example, by statute, all government unit heads within the OIG's jurisdiction are required to cooperate with the office and make all necessary employees and documents available to OIG staff. Further, the OIG is granted access to all documents maintained by public contractors and public grantees.[62] Access is granted even if documents are confidential, and further, OIG documents are confidential unless required to be made public in the course of performing statutory duties.[63] Also, the IG has subpoena power, called *summons power* in Massachusetts, for documents.[64] The OIG may also summon individuals for sworn testimony, but to do so it must comply with a much more cumbersome process than is required for documents. Here, the OIG is required to petition for permission from the IG council, a statutory body made up of the four constitutional officers of the state and five appointees, and it must receive approval from three-fourths of the council.[65] The only area where the Massachusetts OIG varies significantly from the archetypal OIG in terms of authority is that it lacks law-enforcement authority; however, it does have authority to institute a civil action to recover funds from a bad actor, with permission from the attorney general, or it can refer such cases to the attorney general.[66]

As for independence, this is where the OIG is closest to the archetypal model. Although the statutes that create the OIG do not specifically refer to it as an independent unit, several other protections to the office's independence from the agencies it oversees are in place. The appointment of the IG is to be made only on demonstrated professional experience and without regard to political affiliation, upon a majority vote of the governor, the attorney general, and the state auditor.[67] The IG holds office for a term of five years, for a maximum of two terms, and can only be removed for a finding of neglect of duty, gross misconduct, or a conviction of crime upon a majority vote of the appointees.[68] Reasons for the removal must be made public in writing and provided to the legislature.[69] Regarding its budget, the Massachusetts OIG derives its budget directly from the legislature, but unlike the archetypal OIG, it is *not* a set percentage of the commonwealth's general fund budget. The OIG submits a budget for approval like any other state agency, with some supervision from the IG council.[70] Nevertheless, by statute, the IG has sole authority to hire, set salaries, fire OIG staff, and promulgate personnel regulations for the office; furthermore, no OIG employees shall hold or be a candidate for an elective public office during their term or employment or for three years after employment.[71] Finally, annual and interim reports go to the legislature, the governor, and all agencies that were reviewed in the past year, as well as to the public.[72]

By contrast, the OIG for the Minnesota Department of Human Services is designed rather differently from the archetype in multiple ways. It was created in 2011 through the agency head's reorganization of staff and, therefore, lacks any statutory legal base.[73] The duties this OIG performs are limited to investigations only and do not extend to conducting audits. Additionally, its investigative duties do not extend to the agency's employees, but rather, its jurisdiction is external, over contractors, licensees, and beneficiaries of the department. A separate preexisting unit—a compliance office—oversees internal activities. The OIG has no formal subpoena power or requirements for cooperation.

The Minnesota OIG has no independence in the sense recommended by the Association of Inspectors General in its Green Book and model legislation. There are no hiring or firing protections for the IG, and the agency head sets the budget, so there is no budgetary independence. Most important is the fact that this OIG is in charge of all licensing duties for the agency, which provides an external impairment to the OIG's independence. Licensing is clearly a regulatory function, not an oversight function. With the assignment of these duties, the OIG immediately lacks independence to monitor one of the primary duties of the department. In other words, the OIG cannot, without bias, oversee the licensing program as it runs the program itself.

In sum, the Minnesota OIG is nearly as different from the archetypal OIG as possible: it has no statutory basis, no budgetary independence, no job security for the inspector general at its helm, only investigatory duties (and no audit duties), few investigatory powers, no protections from retaliation, and its independence is compromised by being weighed down with regulatory duties in addition to oversight duties. This is not to say that within these confines the OIG is not improving accountability and performance. In fact, it has identified weaknesses in both home childcare and methadone programs and suggested legislation to fix these problems, which were passed by the Minnesota legislature.[74]

The examples from Massachusetts and Minnesota provide stark contrasts in the design of state-level OIGs. Which is more typical, Massachusetts or Minnesota? How much do other states adhere to the archetypal model? How much do they depart from it, and why? Data from my survey help to answer this question.

Beginning with legal form, of the 159 OIGs surveyed, 68 percent were established formally through statute or ordinance, whereas the remaining 32 percent were established by a discretionary act. Put another way, while two-thirds of these OIGs are designed in keeping with the statutory element of the archetype, a full one-third of state and local OIGs lack a basis for legal existence and can be eliminated at any time at the discretion of a policy leader. These patterns vary between state-level OIGs and local or multijurisdictional OIGs. While three-fourths of state-level OIGs have been created in statute, only a little more than half (52 percent) of local and multijurisdictional OIGs were established by statute.

The nature of the discretionary act that creates an OIG varies as well, as is illustrated in tables 3.1 to 3.3. These tables provide survey respondents' an-

Table 3.1. Survey Question: Which of the Following Best Describes the Discretionary Legal Form of the Establishment of Your OIG? Answers from All Respondent OIGs

	Response	%
The OIG was established under an agency head's discretion	11	42
The OIG was established by the executive leader by written executive order	8	31
The OIG was established under the executive leader's discretion, but not by written executive order	3	12
Other	4	15
Total	26	100

Table 3.2. Survey Question: Which of the Following Best Describes the Discretionary Legal Form of the Establishment of Your OIG? Answers from State OIGs

	Response	%
The OIG was established under an agency head's discretion	10	53
The OIG was established by written executive order	6	32
The OIG was established under the executive leader's discretion, but not by written executive order	2	10
Other	1	5
Total	19	100

swers to a question about their OIG's discretionary legal form. The first table includes the responses from all OIG respondents (table 3.1); the second (table 3.2) and third tables (table 3.3) break out the data according to whether the respondents are on the state level or from the local and multijurisdiction respondents.

Although the number of cases is small for this survey question, these data show that the most common discretionary action creating a state-level OIG is from the agency head. This approach has the least permanence, and therefore protects an OIG's basis of authority the least, as is it well within an agency head's discretion to reorganize his or her staff. The second most common legal form for state OIGs is an executive order by a governor or mayor, which provides more protection to an OIG than action by an agency head. Although a governor or mayor's authority to issue an executive order comes out of the same discretionary authority an agency head has to reorganize an agency, the reversal of an executive order requires a public announcement. The political ramifications of doing away with an OIG created by executive order in the eyes

Table 3.3. Survey Question: Which of the Following Best Describes the Discretionary Legal Form of the Establishment of Your OIG? Answers from Local/Multijurisdictional OIGs

	Response	%
The OIG was established under an agency head's discretion	1	17
The OIG was established by written executive order	2	33
The OIG was established under the executive leader's discretion, but not by written executive order	1	17
Other	2	33
Total	6	100

Table 3.4. Activities Pursued by OIGs

	Both (%)	Investigations (%)	Audits (%)	Total
All OIGs	107 (67)	47 (30)	5 (3)	159
State OIGs	71 (65)	35 (32)	3 (3)	109
Local/multijurisdictional OIGs	36 (72)	12 (24)	2 (4)	50

of the public would discourage a reversal. Respondents from local and multijurisdictional OIGs indicated that executive orders were the most common form of discretionary establishment.

How often are state and local OIGs designed to perform both *audits* and *investigations*, as advised by the archetype? As shown in table 3.4, 67 percent follow the archetype model of performing both audits and investigations, while 30 percent performed only investigations. The minority of OIGs, 3 percent, perform only audits. Local and multijurisdictional OIGs tend to conform to the archetype and perform both investigations and audits more often than state OIGs, although the difference is not great.

Additionally, twelve respondents reported that their OIGs perform activities other than audits, investigations, or evaluations. These respondents include seven state-level OIGs and five local OIGs. Like the Minnesota OIG, these twelve are potentially weighed down with duties that may hamper their role of collecting unbiased information for the accountability process. In table 3.5, these additional duties are listed and categorized as consistent with oversight or inconsistent with oversight. The table does not indicate this, but the local OIGs' extra activities were all consistent with archetypal OIG oversight, while some state OIGs reported performing activities that appear to be inconsistent with the archetype. Without more detail about these activities than was provided in the survey, I cannot be sure whether the duties constitute an external impairment to independence (i.e., the OIG's participation results in the OIG's inability to provide an impartial assessment). Nevertheless, certain duties, because of their programmatic or regulatory nature, appear to be directly inconsistent with the concept of OIG independence.

How much does the design of state and local OIGs follow the archetype regarding specific authority to carry out the OIG mission? Of the responding OIGs, 72 percent report that they have subpoena power or other authority to compel cooperation. Although the extent of this authority is not specified (i.e., who is required to cooperate with the OIG and whether the OIG has authority to compel both record and testimony), these OIGs generally seem to have formal authority to gather the information they need to perform their

Table 3.5. Survey Question: What Activities Does Your OIG Perform Besides Investigations, Audits, and Evaluations?

Other duties that appear *consistent* with oversight:
- Complaint intake and reporting (two respondents)
- Coordination of external audits, investigations, and reviews (two respondents)
- Ethics guidance, formal and informal (four respondents)
- Inspections (two respondents)
- Policy and procedure recommendations and other technical assistance to management (three respondents)
- Referrals to law enforcement (one respondent)
- Reviews of trust account activities (one respondent)
- Training on corruption, error reduction, and ethics (three respondents)

Other duties that appear *inconsistent* with oversight:
- Administrative sanctions, suspensions, terminations, and/or appeals (two respondents)
- Development of an automated security system (one respondent)
- Licensing (one respondent)
- Special projects (one respondent)
- Technical assistance for out-of-state criminal background checks (one respondent)

Total responses: 12

oversight duties. Nonetheless, nearly 28 percent of OIGs lack any authority to compel disclosure of information. On this matter, state and local-level or multijurisdictional OIGs do not seem to differ significantly, although fewer local and multijurisdictional OIGs have this authority. Specifically, 76 percent of state-level OIGs and 62 percent local and multijurisdictional OIGs have some authority to compel cooperation with their work.

Finally, there is large variation in OIGs' levels of independence. For example, one key way that an OIG's independence is protected is through a grant of autonomy to the OIG to determine which issues to audit or investigate. Without this grant of autonomy, the OIG's work can be directed by those who have a political stake in the outcome of the OIG's work product. Most survey respondents noted that they have full authority to audit or investigate without interference from the agency or agencies they oversee; however, 14 percent (of an *n* of 51) lack that independence, as shown in table 3.6. Also shown is the breakdown of responses from state OIGs versus the local and multijurisdictional OIGs. A higher percentage of local and multijurisdictional OIGs have this aspect of independence than do state OIGs.

OIGs also vary in the extent to which they have budgetary independence from the agency that is overseen. The manner in which the OIG is protected from budgetary retaliation in response to an audit or investigation may be a

Table 3.6. Survey Question: How Broad Is Your OIG's Authority to Determine What to Investigate or Audit?

	Response	%
Answers from all OIGs		
Full authority, without any interference from the agency/ agencies that your OIG oversees	46	87
Less than full authority, subject to direction from the agency/ agencies that your OIG oversees	7	13
Total	53	100
Answers from state OIGs only		
Full authority, without any interference from the agency/ agencies that your OIG oversees	31	84
Less than full authority, subject to direction from the agency/ agencies that your OIG oversees	6	16
Total	37	100
Answers from local/multijurisdictional OIGs		
Full authority, without any interference from the agency/ agencies that your OIG oversees	14	93
Less than full authority, subject to direction from the agency/ agencies that your OIG oversees	1	7
Total	15	100

flat percentage of the general fund of the agency that is overseen, as is proposed in the Association of Inspectors General's model legislation, or a method by which the agency that is overseen is not setting the budget for the OIG. Frequently, this protection is provided when an OIG's budget is appropriated directly from the legislative body. Less than half—44 percent, to be precise—of OIGs of 149 survey respondents reported they have budgetary independence from the entities they oversee. Budgetary independence is much greater in local and multijurisdictional OIGs than state OIGs: 62 percent of local and multijurisdictional respondents report some type of budgetary independence, while only 35 percent of state-level OIGs report the same.

A third type of independence relates to the appointment of the IG. The archetype recommends an appointment process that is not under the discretionary control of the agency being overseen. In some locations, this hiring independence is maintained with an IG's appointment by an entity external to the agency to be overseen. Other jurisdictions have a statute that requires the IG be hired on the basis of his or her professional qualifications, and others require external confirmation of the appointment by an entity such as a senate.

Table 3.7. Differences in Independence between State and Local OIGs

Independence index (0 is low, 3 is high)	State (%)	Local (%)	Total (%)
0	11 (11)	11 (25)	22 (15)
1	47 (46)	5 (11)	52 (36)
2	16 (16)	7 (16)	23 (16)
3	27 (27)	21 (48)	48 (33)
Total number of OIGs	101	44	145

Regarding this type of independence, just over half of the OIGs have hiring protections. Out of 155 respondents, 53 percent reported some type of hiring protection, such as those mentioned above, while the remaining 47 percent lacked any such protections. In this aspect, local and multijurisdictional OIGs (74 percent) have more independence than state-level OIGs (43 percent).

To understand the adherence to and deviation from the archetype across the universe of state and local OIGs, I created a simple additive index on three key characteristics of independence: statutory creation, budgetary independence, and hiring protections for the IG. This independence index ranges from zero to three. If an OIG reported having all three protections, they rank a three, but if it has none of these protections it ranks a zero. Table 3.7 shows that nearly the majority of state-level OIGs, almost 50 percent, have only one of these protections available. Only a little more than 25 percent have all three indicators of independence. Although there are fewer local OIGs, the data show that they are generally more independent, with nearly 50 percent having all three indicators of independence. The local OIG independence is not surprising as the government structure is less complex. Many of the local IGs are appointed by a city or county council and get their budget from that source rather than from the mayor or the city manager, which provides them with two points on this index.

The data in table 3.7 reveal considerable deviation from the archetypal model of OIG independence. Local OIGs generally appear to be more similar to the archetype than state-level OIGs. Many state-level OIGs have only one or none of these three attributes of independence favored by the archetype. Although there are other ways to support an OIG's independence and its ability to produce unbiased, reliable information than just these three methods of statutory creation, budgetary independence, and IG hiring protections, they are widely regarded as key conditions for effective OIG independence. In sum, design variations potentially undercut an OIG's ability to do its job.

What Is the Source of These Variations?

As noted in the introductory chapter, studies on the diffusion of innovation identify several sources of variation in policy design. Perhaps the most important of these is reinvention, or customization, that results from policymakers' adjustments of common models to address local conditions.[75] This explanation seems to describe some of the variations in OIG design. Nonetheless, much of the variation in OIG design seems to result from another consideration: policymakers' deliberate effort to undermine the effectiveness of OIGs.

The Minnesota case, although a dramatic deviation from the archetype, ironically illustrates the first pattern: adaptation of the common model to fit local conditions. This benign customization occurs in a state that has experienced low numbers of corruption convictions over time and fairly even competition between the two major political parties. The state's single OIG, which is described at the beginning of this chapter, is found in the Department of Human Services. Before its adoption, governor-elect Mark Dayton had run on a campaign pledge to increase government transparency and performance. The governor appointed Lucinda Jesson as commissioner of the Department of Human Services and, following the governor's lead, she announced a plan to increase accountability, fraud prevention, and recovery through the creation of an OIG.[76] The public announcement of the OIG noted that the commissioner had been influenced by federal OIGs and other state OIGs in the area of human services.[77]

Although Commissioner Jesson was firmly committed to having an effective OIG, her design choices—establishment of the OIG by discretionary reorganization, without legal authority and independence, focused only on investigations and not audits, and mixing regulation (licensing) with oversight—reflected pragmatic adaptations to existing Minnesota governing structures and policies.[78] The decision to establish the office by means of her discretion rather than pursing an executive order or statute resulted from an interest to move quickly after her appointment to consolidate the agency's existing fraud investigators who were located in individual program units across the agency.[79] The decision to include the regulatory licensing unit in the new OIG was a result of her learning that the head of licensing was concerned about the limitations of using licensing sanctions to address fraud.[80] He had concerns, for instance, that if a licensee was found in violation of licensing requirements, the licensing unit could only take administrative action against the license. Meanwhile, the licensee could continue receiving payments from the state for substandard service. As his ideas to address these issues were in line with the commissioner's concerns about program integrity, she asked him to become the first IG and brought the agency's licensing staff into the OIG.[81]

The decision to craft the OIG's jurisdiction to include monitoring of contractors, licensees, and beneficiaries but not department employees was an effort to avoid turf battles.[82] At the time the OIG was created, the department already had an internal compliance unit, tasked with determining employees throughout the agency were in compliance with applicable laws and regulations, and an internal audit office, which examined and evaluated the department's fiscal and program management.[83] Thus, the OIG was crafted to provide a different focus than already existed.

The unique combination of the commissioner's vision, the licensing director's interest, and the existing compliance and auditing functions resulted in a uniquely designed OIG in Minnesota. Despite its deviation from the OIG archetype, it has been well received in the state and within the department.[84] Further, the OIG has spearheaded multiple legislative amendments to improve the department's oversight over external stakeholders.[85]

Another example of localized needs shaping the design of an OIG is found in the OIG for the Illinois Department of Human Services. This OIG, which is one of many in the state of Illinois, has many characteristics of the archetypal OIG. It is created in statute; has subpoena powers for documents and testimony; has access to any facility, agency, or employee within its jurisdiction; has an IG appointed by the governor for a term of four years; and line-item appropriation from the Illinois General Assembly.[86] Still, this Illinois OIG differs from the archetype in one key way: it has a very narrow statutory mission, to investigate allegations of abuse, neglect, or financial exploitation of adult individuals receiving services in state facilities or agencies licensed by the department.[87] It also investigates any deaths of individuals in these facilities.[88] The statute that creates the OIG specifically states the OIG has *no* oversight over the routine programmatic, licensing, and certification operations of the department.[89]

This unique jurisdiction was created to address a very particular concern of the Illinois General Assembly, that older citizens were being exploited and the department was not effectively addressing the issue with its internal investigations unit.[90] A task force report prepared for the department exposed poor conditions in the state's twenty-one institutions, including "patients . . . starved, beaten, sexually assaulted, locked in bathrooms, tied to toilets and had alcohol poured into open wounds."[91] The department's director responded to the report by creating an internal OIG.[92] Advocacy groups complained about this action stating: "Instead of addressing the underlying problem of abuse, all they are doing is reorganizing within the department,"[93] and "throwing more millions of dollars at the large institutions or tightening up on procedures is not the answer."[94] These groups lobbied for an independent OIG, whose work would be open for public review.[95] As a result, the Illinois legislature (the General Assembly) created the OIG in 1987 to investigate suspected abuse or neglect.[96] In sum, this OIG's narrow jurisdiction is directly the result of the need to address a specific local problem.

In contrast to these examples, other instances of deviation from the archetype OIG seem based on a desire to undermine its effectiveness. In these cases, concerns about the potential power of an archetypal OIG result in design characteristics that lessen the ability of the OIG to do its job. In the following pages I will summarize a number of examples of deliberate efforts to limit the independence or authority of OIGs at the design stage. In doing so, I will consider whether these efforts are more likely in states (or cities) with high levels or traditions of corruption (where we might expect powerful actors to fight to limit the power of an OIG). I will also consider whether these efforts are more likely in states (or cities) strongly controlled by one or the other political party (where powerful actors may want to limit the authority of an agency like an OIG that has an independent base of power). Ultimately, the evidence does not support either of these hypotheses. These design choices aimed at undercutting the independence or authority of OIGs are made in states with high and low levels of corruption (as measured by conviction rates) and states with Republican and Democratic control as well as states with divided party control. Instead, efforts to weaken an OIG at the design stage seem somewhat idiosyncratic, based on somewhat unpredictable political dynamics in each setting.

Simple evidence of the foregoing point is the absence of any clear correlation at the state level between my index of OIG independence and my measures of corruption and party control. (For states with more than one OIG, I summed the index scores for all OIGs and divided by the number of OIGs to produce a state average OIG independence score.) The n of states with state-level OIGs at the time of the survey was thirty. The Pearson correlation coefficient between this state-level OIG independence score and level of corruption (measured by federal conviction rate) is 0.26, and is far from statistically significant. The correlation coefficient between OIG independence and the Ranney measure of party dominance is −0.15, again far from statistically significant. Nor is there a significant correlation with the "folded" Ranney Index (calculated as $1 - |[0.5 - Ranney]|$), which measures the level of single-party dominance of state government, whether it be by Democrats or Republicans;[97] the Pearson correlation with this variable is −0.01.

One example of an effort to weaken an OIG's design is from Massachusetts. This OIG, as described above, follows the archetypal model closely except in certain key respects. I will now describe the source and context for these key deviations, but it is important to note that Massachusetts has been historically dominated by the Democratic Party and has had moderate levels of public corruption—neither very high, like Louisiana, nor very low, like Minnesota—as measured by the rate of federal convictions for public corruption. As was described in the previous chapter, the OIG was adopted by the state legislature (the General Court) in the wake of a major public construction scandal. The Ward Commission, which was established to investigate the problem, exposed a statewide culture of extortion for campaign donations in exchange for public contracts.[98] The OIG was one of several reform methods suggested by the Commission.[99]

The Ward Commission completed its final report following the passage of the OIG legislation, and it sharply criticized the General Court's design decisions regarding the OIG.[100] These criticisms document how legislators' fears of OIG power motivated it to weaken the design in key ways. To be sure, the Massachusetts OIG was established by statute, had several appropriate powers to do its job, and had many protections to its independence—all key elements of the archetypal OIG. Nonetheless, the Ward Commission was quite frustrated that the General Court had exempted itself and its documents from the subpoena powers of the OIG as it had recommended.[101] Indeed, the legislature and its campaign fundraising practices were implicated in the corrupt practices documented by the Ward Commission.[102] The Commission noted that the amendments to exempt the legislature were written into the bill in a senate back office between the second and third readings of the bill in the second house.[103] The provisions never had a public hearing, and despite the best efforts of the Commission and its staff no one seemed to be able to explain how these amendments came about.[104]

It is important to acknowledge that the Ward Commission's proposal to grant the OIG power to investigate not only state agencies but also the Massachusetts legislature itself was in some respects radical. By granting an executive agency investigative authority over the legislature it would have introduced novel checks in the traditional concept of the separation of powers (and to some eyes this might amount to a significant revision of this structure). But it is equally important to note that the Ward Commission thought this innovation necessary to address a major corruption scandal in Massachusetts. Whichever view one takes, it is clear that the Massachusetts legislature's decision to strike this key element from the legislation undercut the OIG's effectiveness, at least in the view of the Ward Commission.

The Ward Commission also criticized the legislature's decision to statuto-

rily prevent the OIG from making referrals to federal prosecutors upon finding evidence of the violation of a federal crime.[105] Under these provisions, if
the OIG collected relevant information regarding a violation of federal law, it
would be unable to provide it to the precise entity that could hold individuals accountable for their actions. Ultimately, this issue was addressed by the
legislature the year following the issuance of the Ward Commission's final
report,[106] but the exemption of the General Court has never changed.[107]

A similar story of a legislative body exempting itself from oversight by an
OIG that otherwise had jurisdiction-wide authority can be found in Chicago
where battles erupted over the creation of a citywide OIG. Like Massachusetts, Chicago is dominated by the Democratic Party, but it has a considerably
deeper tradition of corruption than Massachusetts. Mayor Richard M. Daley
proposed the creation of the city's OIG to replace the existing Office of Municipal Investigations, a unit that lacked an independent director, subpoena
power,[108] and authority to investigate contractors and city council members.[109]
When the city council considered the proposal, it agreed to all of these elements but balked at giving the OIG jurisdiction over the council.[110] Aldermen
stated that they were concerned the office's power could be abused for political purposes.[111]

In Chicago, unlike Massachusetts, this objection by the council was met
with a public outcry that demanded more independent oversight over the aldermen and their staff. At that point, the council begrudgingly created what
was known as the Office of the Legislative Inspector General.[112] This new office,
which clearly had a mission of oversight, was required to follow very restric-
tive investigatory procedures, which were carefully designed by the city council.[113] Although this OIG had several characteristics that would be considered
consistent with the archetypal model, such as the hiring and firing protections
recommended in the Association of Inspectors General's model legislation,[114]
the IG could not investigate unless upon a sworn complaint.[115] The problem
with this requirement is that many potential complainants may not be willing
to come forward if they cannot make an anonymous complaint against powerful aldermen. Additionally, the OIG had to get approval from the board of
ethics to pursue a full-blown investigation, who had to find reasonable cause
in the complaint, and criminal investigations were prohibited.[116] The Chicago
Legislative OIG provides a good example of an OIG that was designed very
narrowly by those subject to its oversight with the goal of reducing its ability
to pursue its mission. As a postscript, it is important to note this OIG was defunded by the city council four years after its creation, demonstrating ultimate
hostility of the city council for its overseers.[117]

Florida provides a third example of an OIG designed to weaken its ability to do its job. Like Massachusetts, it occurred in the context of moderate levels of corruption but, unlike Massachusetts, it occurred in a state characterized by stiff party competition for control of the reigns of state government. The state of Florida has an extensive system of state OIGs that dates to 1994.[118] That year, the Florida legislature adopted a law that places an OIG in every state agency.[119] This law was passed on the urging of then-governor Lawton Chiles, a former US senator who was familiar with the federal OIG system and wanted to implement it in Florida.[120] Yet, the Florida OIGs were designed to have considerably less independence than the federal OIGs. Specifically, as initially designed, Florida OIGs lacked the budgetary independence and appointment protections that the federal OIGs had, and their reports did not go to anyone besides the agency head. When I asked an IG who was present in the legislature's chamber when it passed the Florida Inspector General Act of 1994 why these changes occurred, the IG stated: "It just didn't work out. It wasn't something they could get sponsored, you know? They [the legislature] already had something [the Office of the Auditor General]—someone they thought was looking after them."[121] The political actors were concerned about the policy implications of this new office and reduced its power in the design phase.

A postscript to the story of the design of the Florida IG Act illustrates the significance of these earlier efforts to debilitate Florida OIGs: there have been ongoing efforts to overcome these limitations. In 2013, the legislature passed legislation that increased the independence of the OIGs.[122] This legislation was sponsored by two legislators who had accounting backgrounds and deliberately wished to strengthen the OIGs' independence.[123] The new law instituted several changes to bring the Florida IGs into closer congruence with the archetypal OIG. IGs are now appointed by the chief IG, an appointee of the governor, rather than the head of the agencies they oversee, and the IG may be removed only for cause by the chief IG with prior notification to the governor.[124] IGs have the independent authority to hire and remove staff within their OIGs, after consulting with the governor's chief inspector general, and are no longer subject to agency control in this crucial personnel matter.[125] Finally, IGs report to the chief IG, rather than the agency head, and final audit reports are provided to the agency head, the auditor general, and the chief IG.[126] The bill was signed into law by Governor Rick Scott on June 13, 2013.

A final example of designing an OIG in a way that limits its independence is found in the Colorado Department of Corrections OIG. Across the period of this study, Colorado's state government was also mainly controlled by one political party—in this case, the Republicans—but it has very low rate of federal convictions for public corruption. Nonetheless, Colorado designed its key OIG much like the Florida OIGs by withdrawing key elements of independence. Although the Colorado OIG was created in statute in 1999,[127] it has little independence from the agency head. It functions more like an internal affairs unit in a police department.[128] This OIG carries out investigations of criminal acts by employees, inmates, and coconspirators; performs background checks and random drug testing; manages sexual offender registration; and coordinates the agency's compliance with the federal Prison Rape Elimination Act (PREA) of 2003.[129]

When testifying in favor of the bill that created the OIG, the deputy director of the department asserted that the OIG would be an independent voice in various department functions.[130] For example, the OIG's participation in hiring staff by completing background checks was useful in ensuring human resource staff were not hiring friends and family. Yet, when he was asked by a senator whether an internal unit, as was contemplated in the bill, could truly be independent, the deputy director brushed off the question. He said that there is always a question about whether any agency can police itself, but in this case, if it seems to be working, then it ought not be questioned. He also stated that citizens seem satisfied with how the department is working, thereby suggesting that independence need not be an issue of concern for legislators.[131]

In fact, the OIG of the Colorado Department of Corrections has never been independent from the executive director,[132] which would be considered an external impairment to the OIG's independence. The IG answers to the executive director and performs the duties assigned to it in statute and by the executive director.[133] The OIG is, however, independent from other units in the department, which allows it to provide oversight of other units' compliance with professional standards and policy violations without interference from those units.[134] That said, it is also assigned several duties that are programmatic in nature, having more to do with performing the mission of the Department of Corrections than overseeing the performance of its mission. For example, the OIG oversees the sex offender registration program, ensuring that sex offenders released from prison register with local law enforcement. Also, the OIG maintains a K-9 unit that is used to search for drugs or escapees.[135]

In sum, states and localities commonly design new OIGs in ways that withdraw key forms of independence and authority from these agencies. Sometimes these withdrawals seem benign in light of the expectations of the archetypal model, but sometimes these withdrawals of independence or authority, or both, seem to be deliberate, strategic efforts to limit the power of an OIG. Neither the benign nor the deliberate variations seem related to partisan control of the state (or partisan competition) or to the level of corruption.

Instead, these variations seem idiosyncratic, related to how particular political fights over OIG design have played out in particular contexts.

CONCLUSION

This review describes the institutionalized design of an ideal OIG—a generally accepted archetype of an office that is designed to provide thorough and unbiased oversight over a governmental agency or agencies. This model has certain characteristics related to its legal form, activities, authority, and independence that help ensure the OIG has a legal basis, can be both proactive and reactive to problems in the entity it oversees, has powers to obtain the evidence it needs to make a fair evaluation, and can operate without interference and bias.

Despite the emergence of this archetype, many jurisdictions have deviated from its core requirements when designing their OIGs. Although some of these deviations arise directly from practical, localized needs, most grow out of political concerns about the implications of heightened oversight. These political concerns result in deviations from the archetype that weaken an OIG's ability to pursue its mission of monitoring fully, and these deviations occur in states with both high and low long-term corruption and Republican, Democratic, or balanced party competition. Many OIGs are created by an executive order rather than statute or ordinance; perform only investigations or audits, but not both; lack subpoena power or other authority that helps it obtain the documents and testimony it needs; or do not have independence from the entity to be overseen.

The adherence to the archetype, where it occurs, as well as the deviation from the model both demonstrate the power of the idea of accountability as embodied in OIGs. On the one hand, the fact that a definitive archetype has emerged, has been endorsed by OIG practitioners, and has been widely adopted demonstrates the general enthusiasm for this archetype as a powerful solution to accountability issues. On the other hand, the power of the idea of an OIG is so strong that it simultaneously gives rise to concerns about the policy implications of its oversight. For this reason, deviations from the archetype result in a weakening of the model. How does this push and pull for and against the idea of an OIG play out in implementation? This is the topic of the next chapter.

4. Phase III: Implementation

Now we turn to the third phase: implementation. After the idea of an office of inspector general (OIG) has been endorsed and the OIG has been designed, OIG staff have the difficult task of doing the job. Most studies of the diffusion of innovations conclude their analysis with the adoption of these innovations. This implicitly assumes that once an innovation is adopted the process of creation, at least for that jurisdiction, is finished. At least with regard to OIGs, as the evidence in this chapter will reveal, the process of refining and shaping the final form of these offices is far from complete at the point of adoption. Rather, this phase is characterized by two opposing forces documented in this chapter: the overseen agency's opposition to this new form of oversight and the OIG's staff activity to defend the OIG's ability to pursue its mission. The opponents of the OIG work strategically to weaken the office or its reputation. OIG staff, in turn, work strategically to strengthen it and protect its ability to pursue its mission. Both the opponents and the proponents of this form of oversight continue their struggles, which shapes these offices.

This chapter explores the challenges that occur as an OIG is implemented on the state and local levels; however, a recent example can be found on the federal level, which demonstrates that pushback against OIG oversight can occur even if an OIG is well established. In August 2014, thirty-six years after the enactment of the federal Inspector General Act of 1978, forty-seven federal IGs sent letters to the congressional oversight committees alerting them that the agencies they oversee were preventing OIG staff from accessing agency records. Subsequent testimony from the inspectors general of the Peace Corps, the Environmental Protection Agency, and the Department of Justice indicated that these agencies were arguing that the material was privileged or otherwise protected and not required to be disclosed to OIG staff, despite the act's requirement that OIG staff be allowed full access to all agency materials.[1]

This struggle between OIGs and those they oversee largely echoes the congressional debate about the role of federal OIGs at the initial adoption of the IG Act. Congress struggled with deciding whether the role of the OIG was to an independent, critical overseer or a helpful, analytical consultant. Some members of Congress (as well as President Ronald Reagan) wanted a federal IG to be a "lone wolf" or a "junkyard dog," policing management, while others preferred to create OIGs that would serve as a "strong right hand" of management, providing a consultant's role.[2]

Today, OIG opponents and those under an OIG's oversight fear the junk-yard dog image of an OIG. They have great trepidation about OIG monitoring and the potential fallout from OIG reports. Most OIG staff, on the other hand, cast their offices as consultants. They suggest that the OIG's role is to improve government programs and to assist management. Both groups use tactics, both adversarial and nonadversarial, that end up shaping the OIG itself.

This chapter explores the strategies used by opponents of the OIG and OIG staff. My analysis is informed by the theory of bureaucratic politics,[3] which posits that institutional policies are subject to ongoing contestation among elite decision makers in and around bureaucratic agencies. Where that theory has sometimes been criticized for assuming that bureaucratic officials act on the basis of a narrow self-interest that is tied to the interests of their agencies, my analysis brings to the discussion a focus on the norms that inform these officials' understanding of their agencies' mission of accountability. Thus, as will be demonstrated, OIG staffers are deeply committed to the normative ideal of bureaucratic oversight that is associated with the OIG concept, and, collectively, have developed strategies to support their office while reducing conflict with those that are being overseen. The power of the idea of an OIG has been explored in previous chapters in the contexts of *conceptualizing* OIG oversight and the *institutional design* of these agencies. This chapter will extend it to the context of bureaucratic politics.

First, I will summarize the nature of the opposition to OIGs during the implementation phase. Second, I will describe the strategies that OIG staff pursue to help support the OIG's role in the accountability process. As in chapter 3, I will consider whether more intense challenges tend to occur in states (or cities) with high levels or traditions of corruption and whether these efforts are more likely in states (or cities) strongly controlled by one or the other political party. Ultimately, the evidence suggests that OIGs in states with higher levels of corruption do experience more challenges to OIG implementation. There is no clear relationship, however, between the extent of these challenges and whether the jurisdiction is controlled by a single political party or is subject to fierce competition between the parties. Challenges described in this chapter occur in both Republican and Democratic dominated jurisdictions, as well as states that have balanced competition between the parties.

CONTINUING PUSHBACK AGAINST THE OFFICE
OF INSPECTOR GENERAL

As chapter 3 illustrated, those who are monitored by the OIG and policymakers are sometimes suspicious of the OIG. In the implementation phase, these suspicions only deepen. These challenges to oversight are so prevalent that practitioners in OIGs often fully anticipate them. One of my interviewees, a local IG, simply referred to these challenges as "expected bumps in the road."[4] Another local IG from a different state reported: "We always have these kinds of disputes—not [that] often, but I'm always up for a challenge, and they know it."[5]

Efforts to undermine the OIG come in two general forms: 1) attempts to reduce the OIG's ability to do its job, and 2) challenges to the OIG's credibility. The first is similar to what is seen in the design phase, but now the opposition is more intense because, at this stage, OIG staff are in place and the OIG is no longer merely a theoretical possibility. Thus, opponents either protest the OIG's jurisdiction and authority in order to weaken the OIG's ability to monitor or challenge an OIG's credibility by calling into question the validity of an OIG's reports. Agencies that are overseen by the OIG naturally feel threatened by the possibility of public exposure and criticism by an entity over which they have little or no control. They fear an unfair witch hunt from an overaggressive overseer. Even though OIGs by design only produce the information that is used by others and, thus, are not the authorities that ultimately hold agencies accountable for whatever this information reveals, agencies naturally feel threatened by the activities of OIGs.[6]

Although a major theme of this chapter is conflict over the role of the OIG, it should be acknowledged at the outset that the majority of state, local, and multijurisdictional survey respondents report that their relationships with key stakeholders are more supportive or cooperative than challenging or openly hostile. The results of the survey are shown in table 4.1. The survey indicates that the most difficult relationship to navigate for OIG staff is with the upper management of the agency or agencies that the OIG oversees; however, only 9 percent report this relationship is challenging or openly hostile. Of those that reported any challenging or hostile relationships, the locus of these external challenges seems to vary with whether the OIG is at the local level or at the state level. Local and multijurisdictional OIGs reported challenges by the jurisdiction's executive (commonly the mayor) or the legislative body (commonly the city council). By contrast, state-level OIGs more commonly reported that challenges came from lower-level professionals or interest groups/citizen advocates. A few respondents from both types of OIGs

Table 4.1. Survey Question: Please Identify the Quality of the Relationships Your OIG Has with the Following Stakeholders

	Openly supportive or cooperative (%)	Neutral (%)	Challenging or openly hostile (%)	Varies too much to categorize (%)	Total responses
Answer: The lower-level professional staff of the agency/agencies that the OIG oversees					
All respondents	43 (84)	4 (8)	1 (2)	3 (6)	51
State-level OIGs	29 (82)	2 (6)	1 (3)	3 (9)	35
Local/multijurisdictional OIGs	14 (88)	2 (12)	0	0	16
Answer: The upper management of the agency/agencies that the OIG oversees					
All respondents	41 (86)	1 (2)	4 (8)	2 (4)	48
State-level OIGs	31 (88)	0	2 (6)	2 (6)	35
Local/multijurisdictional OIGs	10 (77)	1 (8)	2 (15)	0	13
Answer: The head executive, such as the governor or the mayor					
All respondents	33 (74)	9 (20)	2 (4)	1 (2)	45
State-level OIGs	24	6	0	1	31
Local/multijurisdictional OIGs	9	3	2	0	14
Answer: The legislative body					
All respondents	26 (61)	13 (30)	1 (2)	3 (7)	43
State-level OIGs	16 (52)	12 (39)	0	3 (9)	31
Local/multijurisdictional OIGs	10 (84)	1 (8)	1 (8)	0	12
Answer: Interest groups or citizen advocates					
All respondents	24 (60)	11 (27)	1 (3)	4 (10)	40
State-level OIGs	15 (56)	8 (29)	1 (4)	3 (11)	27
Local/multijurisdictional OIGs	9 (69)	3 (23)	0	1 (8)	13

reported challenging relationships with the upper management of the entities they oversee.

Despite this rosy report, interviewees report episodic challenges to their office and their work that goes to the heart of their ability to do their job. These episodes, while infrequent or alternatively more frequent when an OIG is initially being established or with a change in personnel, are quite intense for interviewees. Understandably, an agency's attempts to reduce the OIG's ability to do its job and challenge its credibility can be taken quite personally by IGs and their staff. Alternatively, these challenges to an OIG's presence are taken as evidence of suspicious behavior, indicating that the agency staff have something to hide and wish to avoid accountability. Thus, these episodes loom large in my interviewees' memories. As the examples in the following pages will illustrate, pushback seems more extensive and sharp in places with traditions or high levels of public corruption. In these jurisdictions, vigorous OIG oversight directly challenges standard ways of doing things, and some officials respond by trying to weaken the OIG.

Reducing an OIG's Ability to Do Its Job

When agencies challenge an OIG's ability to do its job, there are three primary targets for their pushback: 1) the scope of the OIG's jurisdiction, 2) the OIG's powers and authority to do their job, and 3) the OIG's access to the tools and staff needed to do its job. I detail each of these methods in turn below.

CHALLENGING AN OIG'S JURISDICTION

Agencies that are presumptively subject to OIG oversight, and/or their political advocates, often resist this oversight by claiming that the OIG has no jurisdiction over them. A very public example of this pushback can be found in Cook County, Illinois, home to a well-known tradition of public corruption. There, the state's attorney to the county objected that the county's OIG had no jurisdiction over her office. The county's OIG was created in 2007 in ordinance by the board of commissioners for the purpose of "detect[ing], deter[ring] and prevent[ing] corruption, fraud, waste, mismanagement, unlawful political discrimination or misconduct in the operation of County government."[7] Individuals subject to OIG oversight include county employees, elected and appointed officials, contractors, subcontractors, and those doing or seeking to do business with County government.[8] This language seemed to include the office of the state's attorney within the OIG's jurisdiction, but the state's attorney for the county objected to this. From the earliest deliberation by the county board on the OIG concept, the state's attorney for the county argued that it would be unconstitutional for the OIG to have jurisdiction over her office on the grounds that the office was a state agency rather than a county agency.[9] The board eventually approved the ordinance against the advice of the state's attorney.[10]

The issue was neither resolved nor addressed until four years later in 2011. That year, the 2004 murder of a young man in a street brawl suddenly became a highly publicized and politically charged situation when the press learned that the alleged attacker, Richard J. Vanecko, was a nephew of former Chicago mayor Richard M. Daley. To many observers, the actions of the police and the state's attorney for the county, who had declined to charge Vanecko, appeared to be a result of political power rather than criminal justice.[11] When the OIG set out to investigate the state's attorney's handling of the case, the state's attorney again rejected the idea that OIG had jurisdiction over the office for the same reasons she had asserted before: that her office was not within the county government, but rather was a state agency operating in the county.[12] In response, the IG chose not to challenge the state's attorney's refutation of its jurisdiction.

The following year, the county assessor, an independently elected county official, followed the state's attorney's lead and refused to cooperate with OIG investigators and rejected a subpoena.[13] The assessor's argument was that it was an unconstitutional overreach for the Board of Commissioners to impose oversight over another elected official. In this case, the IG sought to enforce the subpoena in court.[14] Two years later, a judge ruled that the OIG's jurisdiction over the assessor was constitutional, and that the agency had authority to investigate the assessor and other independently elected county officials and their staff.[15] Thus, the jurisdiction of the Cook County OIG was shaped by the actions of both the state's attorney and the assessor during implementation.

Another method to challenge an OIG's jurisdiction is to claim the OIG has oversight over only particular kinds of governmental actions and not others. For example, one local IG told me that those under the OIG's oversight claim his office may only investigate ethics violations, but not incidents of fraud, waste, or abuse.[16] This critique rests on a narrow interpretation of the OIG's statutory authority, which is to "receive and register complaints alleging *misconduct* against [those within the OIG's jurisdiction]."[17] The IG favors a broader interpretation of the term "misconduct." In this case, the dispute has not yet been resolved.

A third jurisdictional argument made against an OIG is that another oversight body has preemptive jurisdiction. In a state with high levels of corruption, an IG who heads a state OIG relayed an incident where the OIG's staff were investigating several high-level appointees of the governor within the state agency over which it had jurisdiction. Staff from the governor's own oversight unit stepped in to take over the investigation, claiming that their authority to investigate trumped the OIG's authority, based on an interpretation of state statutes.[18] In the course of this conflict, the governor's staff confiscated the agency OIG's computers. The conflict seemed to be triggered by allegations that one of the OIG's staff had leaked news of the investigation to the press, which ultimately proved to be untrue. The state's ethics commission, an external body to both the OIG and the governor's oversight unit, backed up the OIG. The commission determined that the OIG had sufficient independence from the individuals being investigated to be objective and, therefore, should not be preempted. Eventually the governor's staff backed down, and the computers were returned. The agency OIG proceeded with the investigation, which eventually led to federal charges of fraud and theft against the governor's appointees.[19]

CHALLENGING AN OIG'S AUTHORITY AND LEGAL POWERS

Agencies subject to an OIG's oversight sometimes push back against the accountability regime by claiming that its authority or powers granted an OIG to do its job are not appropriately exercised. For example, a local IG in a city with a reputation for corruption told me that when his office was newly formed, the agency they oversaw resisted providing the OIG with virtually every document that the OIG staff asked for, including pictures of agency employees.[20] The agency claimed that the OIG had no authority to demand these documents, despite the wording of the authorizing legislation, which provided that the OIG had the authority to "request information related to an investigation from any employee, officer, agent or licensee of the [jurisdiction]."[21]

Another local IG, in another city with a reputation of corruption, explained that critics of his office claim that he can only perform narrow, reactive investigations. He stated:

> That's a point of contention here in the [jurisdiction] so far. My interpretation of the statute is that there is nothing preventing me from looking at doing an audit or being proactive, which I think is essential for any inspector general position. I think that is exactly what the position is designed for—to be proactive. Unfortunately, the way this law is written, you'll see the vagueness in it and the not-so-clear language. And so that has been a contention, whether I can be more proactive or not. There are some that believe I should only be reactive, and so a complaint will have to come through the door, but I disagree with that view. But at the same time, I operate within the boundaries of the law. We will not violate any rules here or break the law. . . . It's a source of contention. We try to do what we can.[22]

The subpoena authority granted to many OIGs is often a particular target of criticism. Subpoena, or summons, authority granted to an OIG generally allows the office to use the force of law to require an entity to provide access to agency records or to compel someone's testimony. If an entity or individual rejects the subpoena, the OIG may take the subpoena to court to request judicial enforcement. Early in its existence, the Massachusetts OIG had to resort to just such court enforcement.[23] After the court—in an unpublished opinion—agreed that the agency in question was legally required to give the documents to the OIG, agencies generally stopped resisting these subpoenas.

More recently, the OIG for the city of Chicago encountered a similar challenge to its authority to obtain documents. Unlike the case of Massachusetts, which, as was just mentioned, was resolved relatively quickly and in favor of the OIG, the challenge to the Chicago OIG was drawn out and ultimately was decided against the OIG in a decision by the Illinois Supreme Court.[24] The litigation focused on interpretation of the following provision of city ordinance: "It shall be the duty of every officer, employee, department, agency, contractor, subcontractor and licensee of the city, and every applicant for certification of eligibility for a city contract or program, to cooperate with the inspector general in any investigation or hearing undertaken pursuant to this chapter."[25] Still, when the OIG asked for documents from the mayor's law department, the department refused to comply.[26] The IG issued a subpoena, which was rejected, and then took the subpoena to court to enforce it. The law department responded that the OIG did not have independent authority to represent itself and enforce subpoenas in court, but rather had to be represented by the city's corporate counsel (i.e., the law department). This argument, which was ultimately accepted by the Illinois Supreme Court, makes it impossible for the OIG to have access to any documents in the law department in the course of an investigation if the law department refuses to acknowledge the OIG's authority to access.[27] Further, it is unlikely that the law department will willingly represent the OIG if it wants to enforce a subpoena against the mayor's office because the law department represents the mayor's interests as well. The Illinois Supreme Court reinforced the mayor's superior position by stating: "Where a conflict of interest precludes such representation [of the OIG by corporate counsel] under [Illinois Rules of Professional Conduct], the dispute is for the mayor to resolve."[28]

Challenging subpoena power is only one way to thwart the OIG's access to information. Another way is much more subtle: to make the presence of an OIG unwelcome. One interviewee, a state-level IG, explained the negative impact of ambivalence on an OIG's work:

> I've seen [hostile relationships between an OIG and an agency head]. Yes, I've seen that. But I think probably, more typically, it would be not that there's a hostile relationship but [that] there's an ambivalence toward the office of inspector general by the agency head which can impact productivity. . . . I mean, if the agency head really isn't interested, you're just cut out. I mean,

you don't get invited to the meetings that you should be going [to], to learn what's happening in the organization. You don't get support from him in areas where you may need it. He may not necessarily comment on any of the reports you send out, so you don't know if you're being helpful or not being helpful, and really, to me, I'd rather deal with an agency head who's happy with my work and says so, or who's displeased with my work and says so. Not getting any feedback at all is the worst of the three options. It hinders the effectiveness of the OIG.[29]

HINDERING ACCESS TO THE TOOLS AN OIG NEEDS TO DO ITS JOB

A third way to undercut an OIG's ability to do its job is to either: 1) fail to facilitate the OIG's efforts to get the staff, equipment, and funding it needs, or 2) take away such essential items. In my case studies, I found multiple examples where it appeared difficult to even appoint an IG in order that the OIG could begin work. In the case of the Massachusetts OIG, the original legislation required an appointment be made through unanimous agreement by the three state constitutional officers: the attorney general, the state auditor, and the governor; however, a year after the statute had passed, the three officers had yet to agree on a candidate.[30] The Ward Commission, which had proposed the creation of the OIG, expressed great disappointment in this result and recommended that the selection be made by the deans of the state's law schools. In the end, the statute was amended to clarify that only two constitutional officers need agree on the appointment of an IG.[31]

A similar story is found in Cook County, Illinois. There, a year passed after adoption of the OIG before an IG was hired.[32] According to the enacting ordinance, the initial IG was to be selected from a slate of three candidates chosen by the Chicago and Cook County bar associations, who were to be helped by a search firm selected by the Board of Commissioners.[33] Some of the delay was attributed to the fact that the bar associations did not like the search firm that the board picked, claiming it was infringing on their independence.[34] Also, some argued that the salary was too low. One board member announced that he would offer an amendment that authorized another entity to select the IG if the bar associations did not offer a slate of candidates within seventy-five days. Eventually, with a higher salary, a slate of three candidates was submitted to the Board of Commissioners.

Another method to prevent an OIG from operating is to prevent the office from getting necessary supplies. Both the New Orleans OIG and the Chicago Legislative OIG dealt with challenges in getting office space and computers. Notably, both of these jurisdictions have long histories of public corruption, and the fights over basic supplies for the OIG reflect an open hostility to this

office that seems common in such a context. In New Orleans, a city staffer req-
uisitioned the OIG's computers and stored them in the basement of city hall
without informing the IG of the computers' location.[35] Similarly, the Chicago
Legislative OIG was not given staff, an office, or even basic supplies.[36] In the
absence of these supplies, the Chicago Legislative IG was reduced to pleading
for office space, using his personal computer, and getting office supplies from
other city departments. In some instances, he paid for supplies out of his own
pocket. He borrowed money from other departments to set up a complaint
line, and he hired part-time employees while waiting through several budget
requests to receive enough funding to hire full-time employees.

Among the most important necessities for an adequately functioning OIG
is funding. Two state-level OIGs dealt with proposals to defund their offices by
their critics. The Massachusetts OIG endured several periods over the course
of a decade in which a hostile governor entirely defunded the office.[37] Each
time, the legislature reinstated the OIG's budget during the legislative session,
even at times providing the IG with a raise.[38] Likewise, the Louisiana state OIG
lost its funding from the Louisiana House of Representatives during the 2012
legislative session.[39] Only following a large statewide grassroots movement to
support the OIG did the Louisiana Senate reverse the decision.[40]

Battles over the funding of the New Orleans OIG, a jurisdiction with a
well-deserved reputation for public corruption, represent an extreme case. In
this case, the OIG was added to the city charter by voters in 1996 but denied
funding for ten years.[41] Implementation and funding came only after Hur-
ricane Katrina shifted local politics due to what New Orleanians call the "Katrina Effect," which caused many reforms to be taken to address corruption in
city and state government.[42] Still, even after initial funding, the staff believed
that future funding was precarious, as it was dependent on the goodwill of
the city council, which had declined to fund the OIG for many years. The
staff helped initiate a local referendum,[43] which is required for a city charter
amendment, that guarantees future OIG funding will be based on a flat percentage of the city's general fund budget.[44] Today, the OIG's existence, as least
based on having the monies to operate, seems to be protected for the future.[45]

Palm Beach County, Florida, provides a final but more complex example.
This jurisdiction, like Cook County, Illinois, has a long tradition of public
corruption. Here, the OIG experienced a one-two punch: an expansion of jurisdiction coupled with refusals to fund the expanded tasks. This OIG was created by public initiative, following several major public scandals, and codified
in county ordinance.[46] The OIG's original jurisdiction was the county government, but a year later, the county board placed an amendment on a public bal-
lot to ask voters of each municipality within the county whether they wanted

OIG oversight.[47] In all thirty-eight municipalities, the majority favored OIG oversight.[48] Funding had been assessed to county residents through the county government, and after the vote, the county requested additional funding from the municipalities.[49] Several of the large cities, including West Palm Beach, sued the county, arguing that this was double taxation.[50] After several years of litigation, the court of appeals agreed with the municipalities and ruled that the county was barred from charging municipalities for OIG oversight, but along the way to final resolution, the court determined, like in Chicago, that the OIG could not represent itself in the lawsuit.[51] The IG noted that the OIG's inability to represent itself in court in this case raises a larger question: Does the Palm Beach OIG have independent authority to enforce its subpoenas? This is the same question that was litigated by the Chicago, Illinois, OIG.

CALLING INTO QUESTION AN OIG'S OBJECTIVITY AND CREDIBILITY

Another method to lessen the impact of an OIG's oversight is to suggest that their work product is biased and unreliable. If the public or decision makers come to believe they cannot trust the OIG's reports about the actions of the people and entities they oversee, then the OIG's influence is compromised. Challenging the OIG's credibility is a common strategy of opponents, whether justified or not.

In Indiana, opponents of the state IG and his office have repeatedly claimed the agency is politically biased in favor of the state's Republican elected officials. Immediately after the state OIG was created in statute in 2005, the legislature's Democrats, who had initially been worried about the OIG's prosecutorial authority proposed by the Republican governor, asked the OIG to investigate the governor himself.[52] At issue was the governor's use of a state recreational vehicle (RV) to attend a political fundraiser.[53] After an investigation, the OIG issued a report stating that the governor's use of the RV violated no ethics rule.[54] In response, the chairman of the Indiana Democratic Party "scoffed at the idea that [the IG] would have done anything but clear his own boss. 'I was shocked that [the governor's] personal political inspector would let him off. This goes to [the IG's] independence and the fact that he is purely an extension of [the governor,]' he said."[55]

In another instance, Indiana Democrats castigated the OIG for clearing an outgoing Republican appointee of allegations of improper travel reimbursement. The spokeswoman for the state Democrats declared: "It shows yet again [that the inspector general] is nothing more than a partisan prosecutor who does the governor's bidding and doesn't act in a fair and impartial way."[56] The next month, the OIG's finding that state lottery employees did not act unethically by attending a Republican political fundraiser was called a "whitewash," an example of "cronyism," and "a joke."[57] The Democratic chairman "said the report made [the OIG] 'irrelevant,' in part because it was playing politics by favoring Republicans and treating Democrats more harshly."[58] The chairman claimed that the OIG had acted inconsistently by finding ethical violations the previous year when examining state contractors attending a Democratic fundraiser. The IG responded that he had interpreted the ethics rules consistently and vigorously, and that this had resulted in more than forty arrests.[59] These attacks on the Indiana OIG's credibility represent an attempt to undermine the OIG's role to produce reliable reports for the accountability process.

In Cook County, Illinois, charges of bias arose upon the appointment of the first IG. The new IG had previously worked as an attorney in the Cook County State's Attorney's Office, and he allegedly had political connections that gave rise to conflicts of interest.[60] A leading local reformer, Michael Shakman, who had successfully sued the county for political corruption in hiring, and against whom the new IG had defended the county in his previous position, threatened to sue the county over the appointment.[61] Shakman stated: "You cannot be a lawyer for a party accused of illegal misconduct in several lawsuits and then take off your lawyer's hat and begin to enforce against . . . clients the very rules your former clients were accused of violating. . . . This is legal ethics 101."[62] The IG responded that he disagreed that conflict of interest would be a problem, but that he would recuse himself from any investigation if conflict arose.[63]

Two aldermen for the city of Chicago, who were targets of investigations, publicly railed against the Legislative OIG.[64] The tone of the charges was quite ugly. A newspaper article reported:

> Embattled Ald. Joe Moore (49th) . . . is still on the warpath nearly two months after Khan [the Legislative IG] accused him of using his taxpayer-funded ward office to do political work, firing an employee who blew the whistle on it, and giving the former staffer an $8,709 payment equal to 81 days' worth of severance to try to cover it up. Moore has tried to salvage his reputation as a self-declared champion for ethics reform—by accusing Khan of violating the law in his investigation of him. On Tuesday, Moore insisted that he's not alone—and that Council dissatisfaction with Khan is about to come to a head.
>
> "There's been an incredible amount of dissatisfaction with the lack of professionalism exhibited by Mr. Khan and his blatant refusal to follow the guidelines governing his office. The City Council has the ability to remove him from office. The City Council also has the ability to refuse to fund his office," he said. Moore said he's well aware that "it can't just be me" leading the

charge against Khan or it would look like he was getting even. "Ideally, it'll be a coalition of independents and others in the City Council who are all united in believing that Mr. Khan gives reform and inspectors general a bad name," Moore said. "The alleged misconduct he's uncovered, even if all true, is such penny-ante stuff, it makes you wonder how he justifies his existence."[65]

Moore's statements were supported by a second alderman who had also been subject to an OIG investigation. He stated: "A lot of people have a lot of questions about how he has conducted his investigations and whether it's been done legally and fairly."[66]

One year later, the Chicago aldermen continue to fight against the OIG's presence. After IG Khan received permission from the city's Ethics Commission to investigate an alderman's campaign finances, the same alderman sponsored a proposal that blocked the OIG from investigating campaign finance issues and placed that responsibility with the Ethics Commission itself, which reportedly stated that it did not want the authority.[67] The Alderman claimed that the timing was coincidental. Rather, he was motivated to "close a loophole" and "ensure there was a review process in place before we got into the next election."[68] Although IG Khan spoke against the proposal as a "cynical ploy" to avoid scrutiny, the measure passed 41–6.[69]

In Richmond, Virginia, opponents of the IG/city auditor leveled charges of bias against the office. Mayor L. Douglas Wilder called the IG "unprofessional" for issuing an audit that concluded the city had yet to implement security measures on gas cards.[70] "Wilder accused [the IG/city auditor] of playing politics, saying he gave $250 to [the] City Council President's mayoral campaign. [The IG] said his wife, a businesswoman, gave the money."[71] The following year, the city council appeared to withdraw support for the IG by ceasing to issue press releases upon the publication of the IG/city auditor's reports.[72] The *Richmond Times-Dispatch* came to the defense of the IG in an editorial that condemned the decision to stop issuing these press releases.[73]

It must be noted that charges that some OIGs lack objectivity are not always without merit. IGs may exhibit bias or may be unqualified for the job. For example, in Connecticut, the perception of the state IG as an overly aggressive and incompetent watchdog led to the repeal of the OIG in its entirety. This OIG was created in 1985 and repealed only two years later. According to the testimony on the floor of the Connecticut House of Representatives and senate, the primary reason was the IG's actions since taking office. Certainly, partisanship played a role in the repeal, as the OIG was an initiative of the Republicans when they were in the majority in the state legislature but who were no longer in the majority; however, much was said about the IG's management of his office. The representative who carried the bill, whose testimony was indicative of others' comments, stated:

> And so we got the office of inspector, soon to be followed, ladies and gentleman, by a series of rather embarrassing episodes. The first of those was the inspector general asking for guns so he could fight organized crime and whackos. And after that, electronic equipment to sniff and snoop, followed by wanting remote-control starters to see that their cars didn't explode. . . . But I might just turn a little attention to some of the casework that was done. You know, last night when we were talking about TAB [the Transportation Accountability Board], the minority leader said TAB wasn't at least an office that embarrassed us. Well, I'm afraid that wouldn't necessarily [be] true for the inspector general.[74]

Arguments were made in response to this line of testimony, suggesting that the behavior of the officer should not jeopardize the entire office and that two years was too little time to judge its potential. These arguments did not prevail, and the OIG was repealed by a vote of 87–52 in the House and 23–10 in the senate.[75]

A second example of an IG having questionable qualifications for the job is found in the state of Kansas. The qualifications of the former legislator appointed to oversee the Kansas Medicaid program were questioned. The *Topeka Capital-Journal* broke the story and pointed out that the IG had neither a college degree nor career experience in the field of insurance, health care, accounting, law, or law enforcement.[76] Further, the appointee had filed for a bankruptcy in a personal business, had experienced personal financial problems, and had been found guilty of a DUI and campaign finance violations,[77] which did not suggest a strong ethical compass. Even though some legislators who supported the appointee noted that he was technically only "acting" IG, because he had not yet been confirmed by the senate,[78] the appointee resigned within a few days of the story hitting the press.

A final example is found on the federal level. Although federal OIGs are not the primary topic of this research, this example demonstrates how an OIG could be manipulated in such a way as to fail in its accountability mission. A recent Congressional investigation found that the acting IG for the Department of Homeland Security (DHS) regularly deleted portions of OIG reports, amended the reports to minimize findings, or delayed issuance of such reports to make the DHS and its staff look good.[79] In addition, he socialized with high-level management staff in the agency and "gave them inside information about the timing and findings of investigations."[80] The investigation began after several whistleblowers stepped forward from the acting IG's own staff and complained about his lack of objectivity. He resigned days before a senatorial hearing at which he was scheduled to answer questions in relation to the congressional investigative report.

Working Collaboratively with an OIG

Pushback against the OIG from those who are subject to OIG oversight is not inevitable. OIGs seem to be less subject to challenge when the upper management of the agencies being overseen have respect for the role of the OIG. For example, in response to my question about a state agency IG's relationship with the head of the agency he oversees, he replied, "It's great, actually. I get a lot of support. She asks me if she's butting in when she shouldn't. I generally do get a lot of support. I work for a really impressive [woman]. . . . I mean, she's sharp as a tack and ethical, too. It makes the job a lot easier."[81]

Another state agency IG explained that the executive director of the agency his office oversaw was a career bureaucrat and she understood and accepted the OIG's oversight role.[82] In particular, the executive director understood the value of the OIG's independence. He stated: "She understands that I'm independent, and [she understands that] if any issues [about her actions or those of her staff] come up, I need to talk with the board chairwoman. And if there are any issues with [actions of] the board, I have to talk with the governor. I don't think there is an issue. I think she understands."[83] Similarly, a general counsel of a local agency overseen by an OIG told me that although he does not agree with every finding or conclusion made by the OIG, he respects the role and the professionalism of the IG.[84]

Conclusions about Pushback against OIGs

In summary, although survey respondents generally indicate good relations with agencies that they oversee, my interviews revealed many instances of pushback against the OIG and its oversight. These incidents arise either from concern that the OIG is a "lone wolf" who is out to do some damage or suspicion that the IG is a committed partisan who is seeking dirt on members of the opposing political party. Ultimately, the extent of pushback does not seem related to the partisan political context. Thus, these incidents have occurred in states that are characterized by energetic party competition, such as Illinois and Indiana, and in states that are dominated by the Democratic Party, such as Louisiana and Massachusetts.

By contrast, the extent and intensity of these incidents of pushback seems directly related to the level of corruption in the jurisdiction. They seem to oc-cur more frequently and become more intense in states and cities that have a tradition of government corruption. Interviewees in states with higher levels of federal public corruption convictions, such as Louisiana, Virginia, Illinois, and Florida, reported more challenges in the implementation stage than those in states with lower numbers of convictions, including Massachusetts, Indi-ana, Colorado, and Minnesota. In several of these cases, political opponents succeeded in cutting funding or other crucial resources for the OIG. These fundamental challenges to an OIG occurred exclusively in places with high levels of corruption. By contrast, interview respondents in Colorado and Min-nesota, the states in my sample with the lowest levels of public corruption, did not report any problems with the implementation of their OIGs.

Pushback against OIGs may be seen as a product of an OIG's level of threat to established ways of doing things. Where an OIG's commitment to clean, honest government is consistent with state or local culture, the OIG is more or less accepted and faces no open hostility or fundamental challenge. But where an OIG clashes with a tradition of corruption, it often faces hostility and direct challenges aimed at undermining its ability to do the job.

That said, intense confrontations appear to be relatively infrequent and seem to be concentrated either in the first few years of the establishment of an OIG or upon a personnel change in either the position of the IG or the head of the agency/agencies to be overseen, when the role of the OIG needs to be newly understood and new relationships need to be developed. Further, OIG staff are on the lookout for such challenges. However, with time, and with the institutionalization of the OIG concept in a jurisdiction, the conflict can lessen. One local OIG explained: "It's a learning curve for them [those being overseen] to really understand what an IG does. . . . You have to keep work-ing—working towards getting a better relationship, getting the job done."[85] The strategies that are used by OIGs to improve relationships with the enti-ties that they monitor are discussed in the next section.

OIG RESPONSES TO PUSHBACK

In the face of pushback, OIG staff act strategically to strengthen the OIG's position in the accountability process and position the office as a helpful con-sultant, rather than a lone wolf or partisan attack dog. Yet, OIG staff must constantly balance the consultant role with their independence and profes-sionalism, which are key to their ability to monitor objectively. My interviews indicate that OIG staff employ four types of strategies to protect the role of their offices. These include: fixing design flaws as soon as possible; strengthening independence; developing alternative methods to get work product to an audience; and building a reputation of objectivity, helpfulness, and professionalism. When these strategies fail, an IG often has to confront criticism and challenges directly.

Fixing Design Flaws

If possible, an initial step is to advocate for amendments to the OIG's authorizing legislation in the first year after establishment. For example, as mentioned above, the Massachusetts Grand Court amended the appointment provisions in the first session after the OIG had been created,[86] ostensibly because an appointment was not possible under the original rules requiring unanimity.[87] In Virginia, the state IG pursued law-enforcement authority for OIG investigators in order to ensure the office had the authority to pursue its mission.[88] Another state agency IG strove to improve her office's independence by requesting an amendment to her OIG's enacting legislation to clarify statutory reporting lines.[89] The amendment ensured that IG would report to the governing board of the agency as opposed to the executive director, which increased the OIG's independence from top management.[90] In Minnesota, the OIG, which is a purely discretionary unit on the part of the commissioner of the agency, pursued a handful of legislative initiatives, one of which assigns a statutory role to the OIG.[91] Thus, although the office has not been formally created in statute, it has been referenced in statute.[92]

Shoring Up the OIG's Independence

When formal steps to strengthen an OIG's authority or independence are not possible, other informal strategies are implemented to increase an OIG's independence. A notable method to improve an OIG's independence is for the IG to be selected from outside the community. To be sure, this is not within an IG's control. In the case of the Chicago Legislative OIG, the individual who was hired as the first IG was from New York.[93] Several aldermen considered his outsider status essential for the IG's effectiveness.[94] An alderman stated: "This is nobody nobody sent"—meaning that the new IG neither had political power (was a nobody) nor was sent by someone with political power (nobody picked him for a partisan task).[95] In other words, the new IG was not beholden to anyone, and this independence was of considerable importance, particularly considering the history of Chicago patronage.

When outsider status is not readily available, as is more often the case, IGs commonly choose office space that is physically separated from the rest of the agency as a means of enhancing the independence of their staff, physically and symbolically, from the agency being overseen. Multiple IGs reported to me that they employ this tactic.[96] One local IG explained the importance of his insisting his office move to separate space. When he launched the OIG, he was located on the same floor as the executive director and between legislative affairs and marketing. This was an inauspicious location, as both of these functions were dedicated to promoting the agency, looking out for its best interests, and representing the agency in the public eye.[97] As the IG stated, these advocacy roles were the "antithesis" of an OIG's role in maintaining objectivity. By being located in close proximity to these advocacy offices, the IG found it difficult to discuss issues with staff who wanted these conversations to remain confidential and unknown to other agency personnel. He also found the location hindered complainants from stopping in to visit. Likewise, interviewees were uncomfortable providing information when they had to walk through the halls in close proximity to the executive director and her staff. As a result, the IG quickly looked for office space that was nearby, but in a separate building. He noted that the new investigators he had hired would be in a better position to do surveillance, if necessary, because they would not be generally recognized by the staff.

To be sure, this IG acknowledged that having been present among the upper level managers for a period of time had some benefits. He noted that it was helpful that people got to know him and to see that he was not a "nasty person."[98] This comment was echoed by other IGs on both state and local levels. Despite the importance of physical distance to help strengthen an OIG's independence, or appearance of independence, it was equally important to be approachable. Some told me that they visit the main office at least once a week—not to catch people behaving badly but to be seen as available to answer questions or receive complaints.[99] Despite having established a separate office, a local IG told me he thinks it is important to understand the "ebb and flow" of the government unit his office oversees.[100] He encourages staff to conduct interviews out in the field, to "carry the flag to let people know we are there," to "develop relationships and put boots down."[101]

Another state-level IG told me that for similar reasons she deliberately located her office at the primary site of the agency she oversees.[102] She finds that her presence is useful to emphasize the importance of accountability and to be on hand to provide preventative advice whenever possible.

Nevertheless, among my interviewees, most preferred to have their office at a distance from the agency's headquarters. A local IG reported that when the chair of his governing board suggested moving the OIG back into central offices in order for the agency to save money, the IG spoke to him about the importance of separation to maintain independence, and the chair reversed his position.[103]

Another method to help shore up an OIG's independence is to obtain separate legal counsel. As indicated by the lawsuits involving the Chicago OIG and the Palm Beach County OIG, noted above, independent legal counsel ensures that the OIG is not dependent on the legal counsel of an agency that is within the oversight jurisdiction of the OIG. Both state and local IGs emphasized that they had obtained permission to hire their own general counsel.[104] The OIG for the Chicago Public Schools (CPS) achieved a similar result through a somewhat more convoluted path. It involves a formal agreement with the CPS legal department, endorsed by the board through the adoption of a formal resolution. While the CPS general counsel will provide legal advice to the OIG, the IG has authority to retain his own counsel if he determines that there is a conflict of interest with the CPS general counsel or with the board.[105]

Developing Alternative Ways to Get Attention for the OIG's Work Product

Both state and local OIGs may enhance their position by developing positive publicity or attention for their reports. These efforts are relevant in light of the nature of an OIG's role in the policy process, which is limited to providing objective, reliable information about the actions of the agency or individual for whom the OIG has oversight. Once the information is provided, whether it is acted upon depends on the decisions of other officials, such as the head of the agency in question. Thus, while an OIG plays an important role, ultimately this role is limited to providing information and making recommendations about how to fix problems or improve processes.

OIGs can improve the chances that their findings and recommendations are acted on if they develop alternative ways to bring attention to their work products. Three methods pursued by OIGs to do so are discussed here: developing relationships with prosecutors, who serve as an alternative forum; providing information directly to the public for action and reaction; and working with the press to create an additional conduit to the public.

Productive relationships with prosecutors are important when OIGs find evidence of criminal behavior. Although a few OIGs, like the Indiana State OIG,[106] have independent prosecutorial authority, most do not. As a result, these OIGs can only be a catalyst to the imposition of criminal penalties when a prosecutor is willing to pursue the violations through the courts. Thus, many state and local IGs proactively build relationships with local, state, and federal

Table 4.2. Survey Question: Please Identify the Quality of the Relationships Your OIG Has with the Following Stakeholders (Prosecutors)

Responses	Openly supportive or cooperative (%)	Neutral (%)	Challenging or openly hostile (%)	Varies too much to categorize (%)	Total
Answers from all OIGs					
State-level prosecutors	38 (90)	4 (10)	0	0	42
Local prosecutors	38 (89)	4 (9)	0	1 (2)	43
Federal prosecutors	37 (84)	7 (16)	0	0	44
Answers from state OIGs					
State-level prosecutors	25 (86)	4 (14)	0	0	29
Local prosecutors	24 (83)	4 (14)	0	1 (3)	29
Federal prosecutors	22 (76)	7 (24)	0	0	29
Answers from local/multijurisdictional OIGs					
State-level prosecutors	13 (100)	0	0	0	13
Local prosecutors	14 (100)	0	0	0	14
Federal prosecutors	15 (100)	0	0	0	15

prosecutors.[107] One state agency IG explained how he believed his OIG's office could be more effective with strong relationships with prosecutors. He said:

> I think we've got a pretty good relationship with [prosecutors in the attorney general's office]. . . . And so they do a significant amount of prosecution of cases provided to them, and some of our investigators are former [attorney general] investigators, so we've got some good stuff going there. . . . In the last two years, we've been meeting pretty regularly with county attorneys, too, especially metro area county attorneys, and trying to establish with them, kind of, that we want to be as supportive as we can in the criminal prosecution of these cases. Because we want criminal prosecution to be a deterrent, and unless there is prosecution, there is no deterrent on that end. Then what we're left with is, the worst thing that happens to these people is that they steal from us like crazy until we catch them and then we tell them don't do it anymore. We're not going to let you do it, and maybe we're not going to let you do it for a while, and then you can come back, because there are all these grace periods in there. It's crazy. We want there to be a little more teeth there. If we catch you with your hand in our pocket, we want you to go to jail. It sounds harsh, but we want that message to get out there. So we

have county attorneys that are in the metro area who are very supportive of our kind of moving forward and establishing some kind of service here that's going to be supportive of them.[108]

Survey respondents report that their relationships with prosecutors are largely positive, as is shown in table 4.2. Data is also broken out by state and local/multi-jurisdictional OIGs, indicating that all the responses that report neutral relationships with prosecutors were from state-level OIGs.

Often, IGs may lend their investigative staff to support prosecutions arising from the OIGs work product.[109] Additionally, many OIGs ensure that their staff are well trained in preserving evidence for effective prosecutions.[110]

The second alternative forum for an OIG's work is the public. Reaching out to the public not only informs the public about the actions of their government but also encourages complainants to contact the OIG with concerns. To encourage the public's attention to an OIG's role and work product, most OIGs develop robust websites that detail the OIG's mission, provide contact information, and post public reports.[111] For example, the Chicago OIG's website provides the following explanation:

> By providing narrative summaries of investigative cases, [the] OIG will better ensure that its activities are more transparent and more accountable to both the city's elected officials and the city's residents. The quarterly reports are intended to provide the city's taxpayers with a clearer, more informed understanding of city government, and to describe [the] OIG's ongoing efforts to uncover and prevent fraud, corruption, misconduct, mismanagement, and waste in the pursuit of a more effective and efficient provision of city services.[112]

In addition to websites, many OIGs develop regular newsletters to provide guidance on legal obligations or ethics rules.[113] Others have adopted social media campaigns. The Chicago Office of the Legislative Inspector General; the Baltimore, Maryland, OIG; the Los Angeles, California, Police Commission OIG; and state of Ohio OIG are among the OIGs on Facebook, and the New York State Medicaid OIG, the Pinellas County Clerk of the County Court OIG, and the Philadelphia OIG are some of the OIGs on Twitter. The New Orleans, Louisiana, OIG has a robust email distribution about its activities.

Finally, several IGs make themselves available to local citizen groups or clubs to speak about the role of the OIG and its work.[114] The IG from Palm Beach County, Florida, explained that she views this tactic as crucial for her office, as the public created the OIG and the public is the ultimate forum for the OIG's work. She also measures the impact of her public speaking. She stated: "We do a before and after [test], so that we can see how much they knew before and how much they knew after. So, we have lots of measures that we look at about enhancing the knowledge base of the people in the county."[115]

Statutory limits on the publication of information can pose problems for OIGs that want to reach out to the public but are prohibited by particular provisions in their authorizing legislation. The Green Book recommends that an OIG should be granted statutory authority to maintain confidentiality of records and identities of individuals who provide information to the OIG, unless this information must be made public for purposes of prosecution or other OIG-related duties.[116] Yet, often OIGs are subject to additional confidentiality requirements in order to protect the reputations of individuals who may be wrongly accused. One deputy IG for a state agency OIG noted that the strict confidentiality requirements initially imposed on her OIG limited its effectiveness, because "nobody ever knew what we did. Only the affected agencies [who received a report knew], but they were obviously not very interested in disclosing our reports or what we found. So, it was very difficult, right, to have some teeth or to get people to do what we wanted."[117] A statutory change allowed this OIG to report to the public general information on investigations that resulted in sanctions, and the interviewee asserted that relaxing the confidentially requirement has led to both specific deterrence of an individual's behavior and generalized deterrence from others who learn about what behavior is problematic.

The third forum that OIGs develop for their work product is the news media. While most IGs prefer not to engage with the press and some actively avoid the press in order to avoid embarrassment for the agency that they oversee,[118] some told me that they will strategically issue press releases to draw attention to significant problems. For example, one state-level IG told me she does not go to the press often but has done so in extreme cases. One time she approached the press when she found that "the department was [endorsing unsafe conditions for state wards] intentionally and looking the other way."[119] Others more aggressively court the press. One state agency OIG explained that his office's findings and recommendations are seen as protecting vulnerable people and freeing up monies for more deserving citizens.[120] He also pointed out that media coverage about bad acts provides a deterrent for others considering fraud, waste or abuse in a way that a single prosecution will not. Another local OIG asserted that change will not arise unless the public pushes for change, and the only way they will know to push for change is if they are fully informed of problems through the media.[121]

An example of an OIG working closely with the news media can be found in a series of articles published by the *Star Tribune,* published out of Minneapolis-St. Paul, called "Day-Care Threat," about infants dying in home daycare in 2012 to 2013. The Minnesota Department of Human Services IG worked closely with the reporters, Jeremy Olsen and Brad Schrade, who ultimately won a 2013 Pulitzer Prize for the series, to provide facts about the OIG's discovery of the problem and recommendations for a solution.[122] The series brought together the OIG's findings with the positions of stakeholders and legislators, which ultimately resulted in legislation changes requiring increased training for home daycare providers.[123] The collegial relationship between the IG and the reporters shine clearly throughout the series, as the IG is quoted in nearly every article.

Building the OIG's Reputation as Helpful

An affirmative strategy adopted by most IGs is to present their office as a valuable partner in the wellbeing of the agency. In other words, the majority of IGs prefer to strike a balance between lone wolf and strong right hand in favor of helping rather than policing. This is a challenge because being a partner must not compromise the OIG's independence and its ability to meet professional standards. As one state IG stated:

> To me, my job is to make the agency head look good, in a way. But I'm independent and . . . I'm trying to make the agency look good, too. Sure, you've got to do audits and investigations, [but] you want to be able to go and evaluate things on an independent basis [in order] to add value and to help the secretary to be able to do their mission, for management to accomplish their mission, goals, and objectives. If you can stop things from getting in the press; . . . the things you can try to help them make improvements [to prevent problems]; that's what you're trying to do is help your agency to not look bad.[124]

This is not an easy task. Thus, another state-level IG stated:

> It's walking on that razor's edge. I mean, you have to be independent in your work, and you have to know that sometimes your work might not be necessarily pleasing for the boss to hear about, but you've got to find a way to do the work and couch it in such a way that you can, you know, retain your position, [and] at the same time you're doing the right thing. Because if you don't, either one way or the other, if you go ahead and do it the way the management team and the agency would like to see it done,

then you've compromised your independence from a work perspective and from a service-to-the-citizens perspective. But if you blindly disregard the perspectives of the agency head, and just blurt it out there and say it precisely and exactly the way it is, you might find yourself looking for employment.[125]

Still, IGs overall emphasize that their offices are there to help rather than hurt. In my interviews, a number of IGs on both the state and local levels stressed this point. For example:

- "We view it as one of our responsibilities not to play 'gotcha' but to look at how things are being done according to the policies and procedures manual. And when we see the need to make recommendations about how to improve it, [we will]. But not to say that you're doing all this wrong, but that there is a better way."[126]
- "The job is not to be the police, not the boogeyman. I want to have presence, not to check up on people, but to let people know me. This helps people ask me questions."[127]
- "Doing annual training helps staff know who I am, as well as the background of the [OIG] legislation and the [OIG's] role. It helps that I am a local guy. I am relatable."[128]
- "That was one of the things that I thought was important . . . to create an entity that was not only trusted and professional, very professional. But the people, the citizens and employees, wouldn't view us as doing our business of the dark hallways of the county government. I wanted to have a face to the office."[129]
- "Well, [we gain] credibility because we are fair. . . . We're thorough but fair. We're not out to get anybody; we don't put cases on anybody; we don't make up stuff. We're fair. . . . There was a case where [I] was asked whether an employee should have been sanctioned. I could have easily twisted some things around and said 'yes,' but we don't do that. We're not the 'gotcha' people."[130]
- "The key is to build credibility. When complainants call, we act on the complaint as soon as possible. [Also we] do thorough, reasonably objective investigations. . . . Now you're always going to have some conflict, as you are investigating people. Then the people learn not to like you because they don't like being investigated versus is it right, when they are a victim or a complainant to have enough faith in the office to call."[131]
- "Our general approach is that we want to work with people, not against people."[132]

- "We are not 'gotcha police.' We do investigations, but we're here to make things better. But also we're here to tell the truth, too. So we—you know, sometimes the truth is not very pleasant. But, that's our job, too."[133]
- "I've always had more of a proactive approach, more proactive in the IG shop. I always feel that's the way we'll move to, being more proactive to help management on the front side instead of the back side [when] you have to do audits and investigations. Try to be more proactive to help out. Be more proactive, and that's a deterrent to fraud and anybody doing things, helping management out."[134]
- "That's what I want to be is fair. You may not agree with the report, you may not agree with what was said, but were we fair in our approach. So far people have been very receptive. We have been very open with them. Any issues that have come up, we have worked out. And I don't think there's any major issues out there that I'm aware of at present."[135]

Building positive relationships takes time. A local IG stated:

I tell the . . . managers, I'm here to add value to your operation, and so you got to get buy-in. There was such fear and rumor about how bad this was going to be [that] it took years, a couple years, for me to calm people down. I said, "Look, you are not going to trust me, because you don't know me. Trust my work product." So, the work product has spoken for itself, and over time, we have built the confidence of the government officials, because they know we're not out to get them. We're here to provide value. Those who don't want to be told what to do, you offer them some value. They say, "I've been in the job thirty years and you can't tell me anything"; you'll never get buy-in from them. They just need to go when their time is up and get out. But for the majority of people down there, they are seeing the value of this service and it's beginning to change, which is great.[136]

IGs use several methods to craft their offices' reputation for being a helpful consultant. One is to work closely with top management in order to create a cooperative rather than adversarial relationship. As one local IG stated: "We measure our effectiveness [on whether] we have such a good relationship with everybody. And to me, it's important. If you don't have that relationship, you can't get things done."[137]

Several state-level IGs in different states told me that if the agency head asks for a review of a program, they make it a priority to review the program and provide consultation and advice.[138] Another noted that his predecessor was not very communicative with the agency, so he deliberately expanded and improved communication. He explained that "without positive communication, it's difficult to suggest change in policy."[139]

Another method for establishing a good reputation is to avoid embarrassing the entities that are overseen. Thus, a state IG stated:

> We're not trying to get headlines on everything we do. We are trying to work with the administration to try to correct the things that need to be corrected, and I think we are fair in our investigations. And people see that. And I've been here long enough to know there are times where people call us and we work things out. . . . [This is preferable to] us just standing on the side firing bullets at people. I think that helps."[140]

Another put the same idea more tersely: "I try to be less splashy for a lot of stuff, although I will testify at legislative hearings as needed."[141] A third IG stated:

> We can work together to get to the right place, but remember that we are independent of each other. It doesn't have to be a fight every time. It doesn't have to be a battle to get to the truth. There are good, honest people that you oversee that will help you and you just have to recognize that. I have colleagues that will fight their battles in the press. . . . I just don't see success in that, other than creating a bigger wall of animosity. It doesn't send the right message.[142]

It should be noted, however, that not all IGs subscribe to a low-profile approach. For example, one local IG said that for real change to happen the public had to be involved and, for this reason, he pursues regular coverage in the press of his office's actions.[143]

A final strategy is to exercise careful discretion in selecting topics for review. For example, one local IG told me that while he views the oversight role as responsive, he thinks it is important not to review every new initiative that management undertakes, because to do so would accentuate the adversarial relationship that can exist between an OIG and the agency it oversees.[144] A state IG referred to his law enforcement background and restated the same idea: "You don't have to arrest everyone."[145] To target issues in a more objective manner, some OIGs complete risk assessments to focus their staff's efforts on programs that are of high dollar or are vulnerable to fraud, waste, and abuse;[146] others prefer to use complaints as the primary source of their work.[147]

Maintaining Professional Standards

Being a helpful consultant does not mean that an OIG may compromise the quality of its work or the ethical and legal behavior of staff. Compromises of these types would diminish the OIG's ability to contribute to the accountability process. These qualities are emphasized in the Green Book. The introductory material states:

> Accountability is key to maintaining public trust in our democracy. Inspectors general at all levels of government are entrusted with fostering and promoting accountability and integrity in government. While the scope of this oversight varies among Offices of Inspectors General (OIGs), the level of public trust, and hence public expectation, embodied in these offices remains exceptionally high. The public expects OIGs to hold government officials accountable for efficient, cost-effective government operations and to prevent, detect, identify, expose and eliminate fraud, waste, corruption, illegal acts and abuse. This public expectation is best served by inspectors general when they follow the basic principles of integrity, objectivity, independence, confidentiality, professionalism, competence, courage, trust, honest, fairness, forthrightness, public accountability and respect for others and themselves. Inspectors general are granted substantial powers to perform their duties. In exercising these powers, inspectors general regard their offices as a public trust, and their prime duty as serving the public interest.
>
> By the nature of their work, OIGs are held to the same or higher expectations than other government officials in using prudence with public resources. Because OIGs often identify and describe wasteful use of public resources by organizations under scrutiny, they have a concomitant duty to conduct their own work in an efficient and effective manner. Office of the Inspector General (OIG) work should adhere to professional standards and include quality controls to assure that all products are of the highest possible quality. This requires an internal quality assurance program and suggests periodic external quality reviews for each OIG.
>
> An OIG is judged by the results of its efforts and the timeliness, accuracy, objectivity, fairness, and usefulness of these results. These are the cornerstones of OIG accountability. Qualitative and quantitative performance measure should be developed, measured internally, and reported to the public.[148]

What do these exhortations mean in practice? A local IG told me she operationalizes these principles as follows:

[I coach my staff to] be polite, show respect, follow the rules 120 percent, because [if] we're going to tell other people what to do, we better follow those rules. I had to fire several of my staff that didn't. All my staff are at-will because I will not tolerate [unethical behavior]. I have a 0 percent tolerance policy.... But I tell my staff, "Be mission focused, do your job and do it well; quality is the most important thing, and you got to produce and get a good return on investment."[149]

The same IG holds herself to these strict ethical standards as well, and she advises:

I think the bottom line for an IG is that you have to have courage, and that is the key, you have to be ready to walk out the door. If someone, in my situation —I don't technically have someone to report to, but I've had in the agency setting—if you are asked to do something that is not kosher, you've got to be able to handle it or be willing to walk out the door. You can't ever question. You have to have the integrity and you can't ever break that because you will lose all credibility. It takes courage to do this job, no matter where you are.[150]

IGs also emphasize the necessity of following the law. All the IGs I interviewed noted that they are very careful to follow the law that applies to their office in order to protect the reputation of their offices.[151] Several IGs reported to me that they have asked for legal opinions from their state attorney general to make sure they were acting appropriately.[152] One IG publicly recused himself from an investigation because he had a prior relationship with the person who was being investigated.[153] Many IGs told me they follow confidentiality restrictions very carefully. In Illinois, many IGs take confidentially so seriously that it hampers their ability to ask each other for professional advice.[154] An IG in another state observed that careful protection of confidential information encourages cooperation, as the parties know that their information will remain within the OIG.[155]

To ensure that their work product is of high quality, IGs may play to the specific strengths of the professional staff, and their own professional skills in particular.[156] For example, if the IG is an accountant or has an auditing background, the IG may focus their efforts on audits. On the other hand, if the IG has a law enforcement background, they may focus on investigations. In Minnesota, the IG for the Department of Human Services has worked in social service licensing, and several major initiatives the OIG has taken address licensees: home day care providers and methadone clinics.[157] A local IG explained the rationale for this approach as follows:

Table 4.3. Survey Question: Is Your OIG a Member of the Association of Inspectors General or Other Similar Professional Organization?

Response		%
	Answers from all OIGs	
Yes	42	82
No	9	18
Total	51	100
	Answers from state OIGs	
Yes	29	85
No	5	15
Total	34	100
	Answers from local/multijurisdictional OIGs	
Yes	11	73
No	4	27
Total	15	100

I didn't want to spend a year doing all planning. I wanted to get going from day one. And so, knowing the investigative side a lot better, even though the [OIG] does have an audit function in the IG's Office . . . I wanted to get the investigations side going, kind of make a name for the office, let people know we're here. And now, if a second term takes place, I think that's where I want to concentrate on, the . . . program audit side.[158]

A final method to help ensure the quality of an OIG's work is to join professional organizations, follow professional standards, and gain professional certifications for staff. As shown in table 4.3, 82 percent of all survey respondents reported that they are members of the Association of Inspectors General or another professional organization. Slightly fewer local and multijurisdictional OIG respondents are affiliated with a professional organization versus respondents from states, as also shown. Table 4.4, which follows, lists the organizations with which the respondents have memberships.

As table 4.5 shows, survey respondents report that these professional organizations affect their OIGs in a variety of ways. Half of the respondents reported strong benefits in the area of staff training; nearly half reported benefits in the area of establishing standards for audits, investigations, and evaluations. Significant proportions also reported benefits in the areas of how to draft written reports and the content of written policies. By contrast, majorities found professional associations to be of little help in the areas of peer review, culti-

Table 4.4. Survey Question: Which Professional Organizations Does Your OIG Belong To?

- Association of Inspectors General (twenty-two respondents)
- Institute of Internal Auditors (seven respondents)
- Association of Certified Fraud Examiners (six respondents)
- Association of Government Accountants (five respondents)
- ISACA (formerly Information Systems Audit and Control Association) (three respondents)
- American Corrections Association (two respondents)
- American Institute of Certified Public Accountants (two respondents)
- Association of Local Government Auditors (two respondents)
- Council on Governmental Ethics and Laws (two respondents)
- National Association for Medicaid Program Integrity (two respondents)
- National White Collar Crime Center (two respondents)
- Government Finance Officers Association
- Illinois Chiefs of Police
- International Law Enforcement Auditors Association
- International Association of Financial Crime Investigators
- Missouri Corrections Association
- National Association of Professional Women
- National Fraud and Abuse Technical Advisory Group
- National Health Care Anti-Fraud Association
- Ohio Investigators Association
- Society of Corporate Compliance and Ethics
- The International Association of Chiefs of Police
- United States Secret Service Electronic Crimes Task Force

Total responses: 29

vating positive relationships with the agency being overseen, internal hiring and firing decisions, and external public relations (with the press or elected officials). In sum, professional associations are seen as especially helpful in the technical areas of the job, but much less helpful in the more political areas of the job.

Several of the IGs reported that they have gained certification as an inspector general, which is offered by the Association of Inspectors General.[159] The certification requires a forty-hour training session over five days, and the curriculum covers issues such as the context of the IG function, ethics, law, office management, investigating, and auditing.[160] The association offers three other professional certifications for a certified IG investigator, IG auditor, and IG inspector/evaluator.[161] These certifications cover the nuts and bolts of auditing and investigation, taught in the same time period as the IG certification. The auditor curriculum covers the audit process, professional audit standards, working with investigators, internal controls, and forensic and information

Table 4.5. Survey Question: How Much Would You Say These Professional Organizations Have Influenced Your OIG in the Following Areas?

Question	Extremely or very influential (%)	Somewhat or slightly influential (%)	Not at all influential (%)	Total responses
Training for staff	17 (50)	16 (47)	1 (3)	34
Standards and/or processes for audits, investigations, evaluations, etc.	15 (44)	18 (53)	1 (3)	34
Written work products and findings, such as audit or investigation reports	11 (32)	18 (53)	5 (15)	34
The content of written policies	8 (24)	22 (67)	3 (9)	33
Peer review	4 (13)	10 (31)	18 (56)	32
Relationships with the agency/ agencies that the OIG oversees	3 (9)	14 (42)	16 (48)	33
Human resource management, such as hiring and firing	1 (3)	14 (41)	19 (56)	34
Working with the press or public	1 (3)	9 (27)	23 (70)	33
Relationships with elected officials	0 (0)	9 (27)	24 (73)	33
Other	0	0	9 (100)	9

technology auditing; the investigator curriculum explores the investigative process, professional investigative standards, working with auditors, procurement fraud, and computer crime; and the inspector/evaluator curriculum addresses types of inspections and evaluations, evidence collection, analysis and documentation, and professional standards.[162] Most IGs I interviewed encourage their staff to become certified, although several noted that they are hampered by funding.[163] Other professional certifications are commonly pursued as well. For instance, an IG told me he was a certified public accountant, a certified internal auditor, certified government financial manager, and a certified government auditing professional.[164]

Although my survey data suggest that OIG staff appreciate professional associations mainly for their technical help and less so for their political advice, there is some evidence that these professional associations provide support from colleagues when dealing with pushback and balancing the consultant and oversight roles. Of course, the Green Book provides quality standards for OIG auditing and investigations, which include topics such as independence, planning, organization, staff qualifications, supervision, and sufficient evidence.[165] Following these standards and undergoing peer reviews every three years helps ensure that an OIG is producing quality work, but networking and candid conference presentations provide peer-to-peer coaching about the careful balancing of being helpful and at the same time being an independent monitor. For instance, at the 2013 Association of Inspectors General Annual Training Conference, the IG from Massachusetts presented on his experience of embedding his staff in an agency for the first time, negotiating those relationships, and maintaining professional standards.[166] A local IG explained the value of this type of networking:

> It's huge. [The Association of Inspectors General Annual Training Conference] is the place where you are among your peers. We all understand the seriousness of the job; the politics of the job; you can talk to people who have been there, done that. All of us have had different experiences, and we share them. It is a place where you can go and be confident that you know somebody understands your work.[167]

At these conferences, presenters convey a common message that this job is tough and to do it, you need to be tougher. Toughness is required in large part due to the conflict and pushback from the entities who are being monitored. Mary Schiavo, former IG for the Federal Aviation Administration, exhorted attendees of the 2008 Association of Inspectors General spring conference to do the best job possible, but to have an exit strategy in the form of an emergency bank account.[168] Other speakers have asserted that if an agency or other entity pressures you to compromise your principals, you need to quit.[169] In short, the profession teaches that it is essential to both focus on doing the job as professionally as possible and making small strategic changes to strengthen the office's reputation as objective, independent, and friendly.

In sum, OIGs widely share among each other information about pushback and how to deal with it. In anticipation of pushback they develop a range of strategies to shore up their credibility and to develop external allies who may help protect the OIG in the face of challenges.

CONCLUSION

As this chapter has documented, after implementation, many OIGs eventually develop fairly positive relationships with the entities they oversee; however, in the early stages of implementation, and with changes in personnel, contentious conflicts between OIGs and the entities they oversee often occur. These conflicts center on an OIG's role in the accountability process, its powers, and credibility. In these cases, individuals subject to OIG oversight who do not understand its role, do not wish to be subject to oversight, or fear the OIG will not provide a fair report fight the extent of an OIG's jurisdiction, its authority, and its presence. As a result, OIGs are thrust into an antagonistic position with those they oversee. OIG staff are required to strategically defend the OIG or, at least, position the OIG to be more palatable to those being overseen. They pursue the role of a "strong right hand" to management.

As Daniel Carpenter[170] observed with the US Postal Service, OIGs gain power and influence to the extent that they are able to cultivate external allies and build their reputation as competent, relevant, and helpful. This bureaucratic authority will also help OIGs deflect threats from opponents and allow them to pursue their mission. In essence, this means that IGs must act politically in order to protect and promote their offices and accountability missions. Doing so, however, places them in an awkward position. Engaging in political maneuvering may erode their reputation as neutral, objective, and nonpartisan, which is fundamental to their role in monitoring. Any damage to an OIG's reputation or even a suggestion of lack of independence or bias may compromise the quality and reliability of the information reported by the OIG. Even if an OIG is successful in cultivating alternative forums for its information, those forums will not be willing to value the information unless it is believed to be valid and truthful. So, while addressing the need to be political and strategic in order to impact the accountability process, OIGs also must constantly maintain independence and fairness.

With the strategies enumerated in this chapter, it is clear that OIGs are creatively entrepreneurial in defending their office and their efforts at oversight. These entrepreneurial efforts include trying to make the OIG's work truly useful—like a helping hand—to the agency being overseen. Nonetheless, it is notable that there is little evidence that OIGs are willing to compromise their unbiased oversight role so as to buy off the opposition. Even—perhaps especially—in the face of determined opposition, OIG staffers are deeply committed to their role as an agency of independent oversight. They are guided in this role by the archetypal model that I have summarized in previous chapters. In this way the politics of OIG implementation is shaped by more than simply the self-interested defense of one's agency: it is deeply shaped by the normative model of the OIG as a key agency of accountability.

5. Conclusion: Are Offices of Inspector General Empty Symbols or Engines of Accountability?

This research has explored the development of a common model of offices of inspector general (OIG), the spread of OIGs across the country, and dynamic variations within this diffusion. As we have seen, while proponents of OIGs hold high hopes for true accountability and oversight, many forces conspire against bringing these hopes to fruition. Put simply, the push and pull over OIGs, from conceptualization to implementation, is best understood in light of the core ideals of the OIG idea as a model to pursue government accountability.

What is the result? On balance, are OIGs effective engines of accountability—or empty symbols? Although, this book does not directly examine OIG effectiveness (that is a topic for a future study), the present analysis suggests that OIGs have helped the cause of accountability despite the challenges they face. This chapter first summarizes the findings of the previous chapters and then explores the broader implications of these findings for the question of OIG effectiveness. The chapter also includes a discussion of the limitations of this research and suggests questions for future research.

The proliferation of the OIG concept across state and local jurisdictions is a story of the emergence and spread of a common, professionally legitimated model of bureaucratic accountability. This model and its spread are best explained by the neoinstitutional theory of organizational development.[1] Neoinstitutionalism suggests that institutions, rules, or norms spread from organization to organization as they become endorsed by a broad professional field as an acceptable way to do things, regardless of whether other options might be more effective in reaching the desired goal. In this case, we find OIGs spreading far and wide across the county because the OIG has become generally accepted as a primary means to address government accountability. This diffusion, from the federal to the state and local levels, is fueled by the fact that government accountability has become a public "obsession."[2] OIGs are held up as a key method to combat fraud, waste, and abuse, and to promote effectiveness, efficiency, and good government.

Throughout the conceptualization, design, and implementation phases, the power of the idea of an OIG as an expression of the norm of accountability is demonstrated. During the conceptualization phase, policymakers who are faced with concerns about bureaucratic accountability have come to view OIGs as the obvious way to address the problem. The very obviousness of this option illustrates the power of the OIG idea. Data show that OIGs are introduced as the answer to a wide range of problems that fall into a broad category of perceived accountability and performance deficits. The OIG gains a place on a policy agenda[3] because the problem stream produces a clear definition of a policy problem, the need for accountability; the policy stream focuses on an OIG as the solution to these problems as the OIG concept has become institutionalized; and the political stream encourages political and policymakers to find a solution for accountability issues. The triggering event that spurs OIG adoption is often a specific, major public corruption scandal, and as a result, OIGs are promoted by a candidate for elected office who wishes to demonstrate to the public their commitment to issues of accountability, or by an internal, professional bureaucrat who sees the adoption of an OIG as an important step to improve accountability and performance. The strength of the norm of accountability is demonstrated by the fact that these OIGs have very few opponents at the initial stage when the idea is proposed and begins to move toward adoption.

These essentially normative and idea-centric conditions are not well captured by conventional, causal explanations of policy diffusion. In fact, data on the state level show that the rate of initial OIG adoption is not influenced by state levels of corruption, the size of a state's bureaucracy, or a partisan dominance within a state. Thus, responding to problems of corruption, protecting a state's investment in its bureaucracy, or the temptation to use OIGs as tools of partisan competition are rationales that have little impact on the rate of OIG adoption on the state level. States are also not directly influenced by recent adoptions of OIGs among their neighbors or the federal government, which has been thought to be a traditional method of diffusion.

After the concept of an OIG has been embraced, steps to give it authority immediately confront practical questions about how it should be designed. For this, too, there is a common answer: the archetypal OIG design, which is expressed in a common form that is found in prominent guidance documents. The archetypal design gives broad powers and independence to OIGs.

It is important to emphasize that the archetypal OIG model also sharply limits an OIG's role in the accountability process. They have no powers of enforcement, no powers of prosecution, and none of rulemaking. Their role is restricted to collecting unbiased information about a governmental actor's conduct and then reporting it to others for action on that information. These others, be they the mayor, agency head, governor, prosecutor, or general public, have the authority to act, but they may also do nothing. To be sure, OIG reports often include recommendations for actions, and these recommendations sometimes shape the authoritative response. These other actors then may review the OIG's reports and call the actor to answer and explain his or her actions. They may or may not impose consequences based on the explanation.

The OIG's limited role in this process is by design. The role is not unlike the traditional roles that auditors or investigators have always had in government. Indeed, the specific duties most often assigned to OIGs are those of auditing and investigating. The role of the OIG is similar to that of fact finders used in arbitration proceedings. OIGs collect information that has otherwise been unexamined, or perhaps has been deliberately hidden, and provide it to decision makers along with recommendations for action.

Thus, the archetypal OIG model suggests that to ensure the credibility of the information supplied by the OIG, the OIG must have 1) the appropriate authority to collect the information needed, and 2) clear independence of the OIG from the governmental actor being overseen so as to not be improperly influenced by the actor when collecting information. Producing complete, objective information is essential for an OIG to protect its specific role as a contributor of information to the accountability process.

The OIG archetype, developed by OIG practitioners based on lengthy experience, has four necessary elements: foundation in statute (as opposed to executive order or other discretionary form), the authority to perform both audits and investigations, the authority to compel access to the documents and the testimony needed to fully collect information, and structural and budgetary independence from the entity that it oversees. If designed thus, the archetypal OIG will have the independence, legitimacy, permanence, powers, and structure that are necessary to perform its role without manipulation.

The research presented in this book shows that the archetypal design both attracts and alarms policymakers: power and independence offer the potential for real oversight, but also for outcomes that are unpredictable and potentially and politically risky. The key decisions regarding the design of a particular OIG are, therefore, often politically fraught. Many government officials would like to maintain a check on it rather than grant it fundamental independence and broad investigative powers, because an OIG has the potential to produce information that governmental actors may prefer to not be made public. This fear is justified because, as emphasized above, OIGs' only real power is to produce information about an actor's conduct. If such information is egregious or alarming that the forum simply cannot ignore it, the forum will be sure to act. Put another way, the OIG's only tool to guarantee government accountability is to shame or embarrass the actor, because the information they produce can simply be ignored. Realistically, shame and embarrassment could lead directly to some direct detriment to the overseen agency, such as reductions in funding for the programs exhibiting problems, but this would depend on another actor besides the OIG taking those steps. Nevertheless, being able to publicize information that is potentially embarrassing is a powerful tool, and in many instances shocking information demands action to correct the problem. For example, if an OIG can produce comprehensive and reliable information that someone has committed a significant fraud against the jurisdiction, a prosecutor will be more likely to charge the individual with a crime, or a supervisor will be more likely to take an administrative action, or a legislator may change the parameters of a public program or reduce funding.

The potential for an OIG to embarrass and shame is precisely why OIGs are so threatening to those they oversee and their allies. Officials under OIG oversight feel this threat even if they have done nothing wrong. These officials, as well as those creating an OIG, fear the unknown and seek methods to control it.

As a consequence, while the idea of an OIG has great popularity and appeal, and this motivates adopting such a body in some form, the same idea can seem very threatening to policymakers and those subject to its jurisdiction. Thus, they tweak or radically revise the design, and the end result is often an office that does not match up with the archetype. Some reasons for these changes are undoubtedly benign. Sometimes a jurisdiction's particular conditions and needs shape the OIG in unique ways. However, it is more common that policymakers withdraw from the OIG key elements of the archetypal OIG's authority or independence. To minimize the potential threat of a new OIG, these policymakers deliberately design an OIG to have a narrow jurisdiction, limited authority, or minimal independence.

Once an OIG is in place, the tensions around the model enter a new phase: conflicts over actual monitoring, whether by investigation or audit, of particular agencies or individuals. Many subject to OIG oversight predictably resist it. The trepidation experienced by those overseen is more intense because the OIG is no longer theoretical, and as the OIG begins its work, those who are overseen by the OIG often chafe under monitoring. One method used to try to reduce the threat of an OIG is to challenge the scope of an OIG's jurisdiction. Another is to challenge the OIG's authority. A third is to hinder an OIG's access to necessary staff, equipment, and funding. Opponents of the OIG also try to limit its influence by alleging that it is biased and therefore unable to provide reliable information for the accountability process.

In the face of this resistance OIG officials are motivated by the model's core ideals to defend their monitory powers, resist erosions of their independence, and carry out meaningful oversight. Yet, these challenges, while intense and difficult for OIG staff to respond to, are not inevitable. When the individuals who are overseen by an OIG understand and accept the role, the relationship can be smoother. Additionally, OIGs can take steps to build a more productive relationship, but this takes time. OIG staff pursue a number of strategies to protect their office's role in the accountability process and build positive relationships with the entities that they oversee in order to reduce conflict and protect the OIG's ability to pursue its mission.

Strategies employed by OIG staff to try to safeguard the OIG and its work product are both formal and informal. An example of a formal method is to pursue amendments to the OIG's authorizing statute, ordinance, charter, or other founding document to correct deviations from the archetype. Another formal strategy is to take challenges to the OIG's authority or jurisdiction to court for a judicial decision. An example of an informal approach commonly employed to strengthen the office's independence, which may be lacking, is to locate the physical site of the OIG at a distance from the management of the overseen entity. Another is to develop alternative outlets, or "forums," for the information they produce to ensure it receives the proper attention. Finally, OIG staff work to build a positive reputation of their office as helpful consultants rather than punitive "gotcha" overseers. To pursue this last goal, OIG staff work closely with management, investigate or audit the programs that management is concerned about or otherwise use careful discretion in selecting topics to study, and work to avoid publicly embarrassing the agency being overseen.

At the same time, OIG staff must be vigilant in upholding professional standards and independence, because if they are seen as too "cozy" with the individuals who are within the OIG's jurisdiction their findings and conclusions will be compromised. Thus, OIG staff make great efforts to comply with laws, rules, and ethical and professional standards, which are considered essential if the OIG is going to review others' compliance with the same. In addition, OIGs try to produce work products that add value. Training staff and joining professional organizations help ensure that the OIG's work quality is high. Communications through networks associated with these professional associations helps to improve training and to share information to help staff deal with the pushback from those being overseen.

Balancing a reputation that is helpful rather than threatening with independence and professionalism is very important. If viewed as threatening, an OIG will have an antagonistic relationship with those it oversees and will struggle to gather the information it needs to perform its role. On the other hand, it is vital that the work product of an OIG meets professional standards and is accurate, because if their work product is considered shoddy or politically motivated, the OIG will lose all credibility. Its ability to provide information to the accountability process will be called into question and ultimately ignored. In the same vein, if an OIG's staff is considered unethical or biased their findings and recommendations will be discounted. Thus, OIG staff must be helpful but maintain distance. They must support the entity they oversee but not become biased. They must not be overly aggressive or embarrassing, but they must produce high-quality information about the weaknesses in the activities of those who are overseen by the OIG. This is no easy task.

LIMITATIONS AND FUTURE RESEARCH QUESTIONS

Although I am reasonably confident in the basis for the brief summary above, inevitably there are some limitations to my data. One is found in the statistical model presented in chapter 2. Although illuminating in some ways, by showing that alternative hypotheses do not explain the proliferation of OIGs it also yielded some counterintuitive and puzzling results. For example, despite an apparent regionalism evident in a visual inspection of a map of patterns of the adoption of OIGs, the results of the event-history model suggest that adoption of an OIG by a state's neighbors seems to decrease the likelihood that a state will adopt an OIG. This is puzzling. It is possible that the model is missing one or more important variables. For example, my interviews suggest that information about OIGs is shared from state to state via specialized networks. These networks may be organized less by geographic proximity than by professional networks that are not geographically based. Developing a measure of these networks would be difficult but, if accomplished, might add important missing information to the statistical model. On this question there is room for further work and refinement.

Another limitation is that the perspectives of individuals subject to OIG oversight were not obtained due to time constraints and logistical issues. Some conclusions about their motives were drawn from their actions, as reported in newspapers and by OIG practitioners. A more complete picture of the character of opposition to OIGs during the design and implementation phases would require additional interviews with OIG opponents and those overseen by OIGs. Such interviews may also help identify missing variables in the statistical model presented in chapter 2.

POLITICIZED BUREAUCRACY: HOW OFFICES OF INSPECTOR GENERAL CONTRIBUTE TO ACCOUNTABILITY

Murray Edelman proposed that many public policies and even public agencies are created not so much to solve a problem but to convey the impression that elected officials are trying to solve it.[4] This may be true of OIGs as well. Put another way, it may be that OIGs are established to make it appear that officials are taking accountability seriously. OIGs may be used to create an impression among members of the public that the government is addressing the problem of waste, fraud, and abuse. Although it might be argued that such symbolism is valuable in that it may reassure the public and confirm support for the values that are embraced (e.g., "fraud, waste, and abuse is wrong" or "corruption is wrong"), it is also true, as Edelman argued, that as a practical matter a merely symbolic expression may bring no change to the status quo.

On first blush, it appears that the diffusion of OIGs may be just a merely symbolic effort to pursue accountability, particularly because an OIG's role is limited to monitoring and reporting. Several of the key observations reported in this book are consistent with this jaundiced interpretation. As we have seen, the idea of enacting an OIG most often arises in the political process and is endorsed by politicians wishing to promote an image of themselves as reformers. Likewise, in many jurisdictions, the initial OIG proposal is weakened or watered down during the design phase so that the resulting agency is bereft of key forms of independence and authority.

Nevertheless, some other observations in this book run counter to this "empty symbolism" interpretation. Although there is clearly a symbolic component to the OIG image, this symbolic dimension has practical consequences in that it motivates widespread support for elements of the archetype that ensure actual implementation, vigorous investigation, and independence from political interference. These particular design features of OIGs and the widespread support for them are aimed at enabling this agency to match the expertise of the overseen agency with equal expertise, and other design features give the OIG the independence and authority to do the job effectively. Although these effectiveness-ensuring features are too often watered down in the design phase, as we have seen, that is not the end of the story. The symbolic power of the OIG concept is also felt in the high level of dedication by OIG staff to pursue the OIG's mission and even to overcome politically enacted deviations from the archetypal model. Nearly everywhere that I conducted interviews, these staff showed a strong commitment to meeting the professional ideals associated with the OIG idea. They emphasized how hard they work to meet the standards, training, professional certifications, and peer review that have emerged as the "nuts and bolts" of the OIG model. Likewise, staff use the OIG model as a way to recruit allies and public support for their mission. Although these efforts at recruiting allies are inherently political in nature, the politics are normative (motivated by James G. March and Johan P. Olsen's "logics of appropriateness"[5]) rather than horse-trading in nature. So, here, too, the normative symbolism of the OIG model is revealed as potent rather than empty.

In employing the normative symbolism of the OIG idea to marshal allies and public support, OIGs become what might be called *politicized bureaucracies.* Unlike a typical agency, it is not enough for OIGs to do the job well. The staff are also required to act strategically—even politically—to overcome determined opposition in highly politicized environments. Daniel P. Carpenter describes a similar dynamic in the U.S. Post Office's efforts in the late 1800s to gain allies and strengthen its portfolio of services and, thus, its budget.[6] What seems different and distinct in this book's analysis of OIG officials' similar efforts to shore up their agencies is the central role played in this story by the normative model of the OIG. This is a case of bureaucratic politics in pursuit of a *normative mission.* The OIG staff are influenced by the norm of accountability and thus pursue the model of the OIG as a way to give teeth to this norm. Although they are tasked with a relatively straightforward mission of monitoring, they face considerable pushback in carrying out this mission and, in response to this pushback, they use the normative symbolism of the OIG model to defend their agency and gain political support for it.

This is bureaucratic politics of a particular type: normatively mission-centered bureaucratic politics. For instance, when OIGs experience intense challenges, they cannot maintain their monitoring role without external champions. These external champions have two important roles. The first is to support the presence and the work of the OIG. For example, if leadership in the entity that is being overseen understands, supports, and values the OIG's monitoring, the OIG can operate with little conflict. On the other hand, if the leadership in the entity that is being overseen resents the OIG or tries to undermine its authority, the OIG can hold out against these attacks and remain effective for only so long. At some point external attacks and resistance are likely to undermine an OIG's capacity and influence. Thus, when the governor of Massachusetts decided to defund the state OIG because he no longer desired oversight, the OIG would have disappeared had the legislature not come to its aid with funding. When the Cook County assessor rejected the Cook County OIG's jurisdiction over his office, there was little the OIG could do until the jurisdiction was confirmed by the local district court.

The second key supporting role of an external champion is to be the receiver of the OIG's monitoring reports. This external champion must be in the position to value the report and act on it. Without a receptive audience, the OIG's basic role becomes irrelevant. To be sure, various external actors can play this key supporting role. If, for instance, an agency head were uninterested in an OIG's monitoring and tried to ignore the OIG's reports, these reports might still gain a hearing if the governor, legislature, press, or the public stepped up and demanded a response. For example, even though the Indiana OIG's credibility was challenged by Democrats in the legislature and its work could have been discredited and ignored, local and state prosecutors found the information collected by the OIG worth pursuing in the courts, receiving convictions in multiple cases. Thus, accountability was achieved in those cases, but if no external authority champions an OIG's reports, they become irrelevant.

In sum, when an OIG cultivates external allies who will have its back, so to speak, this becomes a political act. In turn, the OIG must produce professional work or risk losing this champion's support. Only with the OIG staff's commitment to the mission and dedication to professionalism *and* appropriate political strategizing, such as cultivating an external champion, can the OIG meet the full potential of its intended role.

Other bureaucracies may become politicized in a similar mission-centered way. One example is a state's vital statistics unit. Their role is record keeping, but the unit has been thrust into many political issues of the day: surrogacy, same-sex marriage, and abortion. In order to keep accurate records, these units must negotiate highly political atmospheres, much like an OIG. There are other possible examples: environmental protection agencies whose staff and external supporters face powerful political pushback yet are motivated to forge ahead by their commitment to the environmental protection mission, public schools whose staff face political skepticism or even opposition yet remain motivated by the public education mission, and so on. These examples suggest many significant questions for further research, focused particularly on how the politicization of an agency's mission both draws out opposition and also motivates allies to support the agency and staff to work harder.

Two other observations on accountability arise from this research. First, although strategic efforts to build allies are often essential, accountability ultimately depends on actions by what I previously called the external forum that holds the overseen agency to account. OIGs may gather and present information, but they also need a forum that *hears and acts* on this information: a governor or mayor who pays attention, a legislature that listens, news media that report the results, and a public that cares. This observation makes clear that many types of accountability mechanisms, such as open-meeting laws, transparency measures, and performance budgeting, are similar to OIGs in that they alone do not deliver accountability. They provide information to the public decision-making process, which is important, but, like OIGs, their contribution to government accountability ends there. A separate forum is required to act on the information and call the governmental actors to explain or defend their decisions. As in the case of OIGs, much effort is being put toward implementing these mechanisms of transparency and accountability. These efforts to provide heightened government accountability can be easily undercut if there is no forum paying attention.

Second, a broader conclusion about government accountability can be drawn. This research shows how adversarial relationships easily arise between overseers and the overseen. Overseers are required to be critical and at times suspicious, while at the same time those being overseen resent having their flaws pointed out and made public. They would prefer to not be told what to do. They would prefer to "steer," rather than "row."[7] Although tensions between the overseer and the overseen naturally arise, ideally the goals of the two should be aligned. Each is ultimately interested in positive outcomes of government programs and appropriate spending of public funds. If both entities could operate as partners who are invested in similar missions, perhaps the adversarial relationship could be lessened and accountability supported rather than challenged. Although some natural resentment may be understandable when someone is monitoring your actions, in the public sector, public managers ought not have the luxury to complain. Instead, their stance should be: "I always welcome the opportunity to do a better job for the public." At the same time, OIG staff should not be heavy-handed sentries. They should understand that most pubic managers are well motivated. If this shift in attitude could occur, the antagonism between public managers and OIG staff could be reduced.

It may be too much to hope for congenial relations between OIGs and the agencies they oversee. After all, the model of an ideal OIG that has emerged in recent decades is of an oversight agency that has the independence and tools necessary to conduct thorough audits and investigations; identify problems with effectiveness and efficiency; root out waste, fraud, and abuse; and publicize the results. In many instances OIGs have performed these tasks admirably. OIGs have provided crucial independent reports on a wide range of issues. Despite the ongoing conflict over the OIG role, it is increasingly clear that these units play a valuable role in the government accountability process and are here to stay.

Appendix A: State Rankings on Two Indicators of Corruption

Average Annual Public Integrity Convictions (2002–2011) per 1,000 State and Local Full-Time Equivalent Employees (FTE)

Rank	State	Average
1	Kansas	2.044020836
2	Oregon	2.161313894
3	South Carolina	2.237245298
4	New Hampshire	2.311543061
5	**Minnesota**	**2.364873331**
6	Nebraska	2.397753461
7	Washington	2.412164186
8	Idaho	2.805677291
9	Utah	2.924181463
10	**Colorado**	**3.071091345**
11	Iowa	3.091914322
12	Nevada	3.426111005
13	North Carolina	3.617387934
14	New Mexico	3.676378797
15	California	3.691144264
16	Wisconsin	3.96673846
17	**Indiana**	**4.138008814**
18	Wyoming	4.456912904
19	Vermont	4.543705727
20	Connecticut	4.649632722
21	Maine	4.731373982
22	New York	4.759696428
23	Georgia	4.873777785
24	Michigan	4.95125554
25	Texas	5.35246332
26	Rhode Island	5.698994158
27	Missouri	5.839227188
28	Arkansas	5.840518746
29	Hawaii	6.198070627
30	**Massachusetts**	**6.412578856**
31	Arizona	6.61177554
32	Oklahoma	6.793499467
33	**Florida**	**7.188741556**
34	West Virginia	7.489992204

(continued on the next page)

Rank	State	Average
35	**Illinois**	**7.675433605**
36	Ohio	7.715853782
37	Tennessee	8.089634436
38	New Jersey	8.522833346
39	Alaska	8.687862811
40	Pennsylvania	8.914181215
41	Maryland	9.108005188
42	Alabama	9.688
43	Mississippi	9.929649585
44	**Virginia**	**10.21430118**
45	Montana	11.05469198
46	Kentucky	12.5301795
47	North Dakota	13.25021984
48	South Dakota	14.49261047
49	**Louisiana**	**18.60076651**
50	Delaware	23.92205221

Note: States in which I conducted interviews are in bold.

Numerical Equivalent of Standard and Poor's State Bond Ratings, Averaged from 2001 to 2012

Rank	State	Average Rating
1	Delaware	25
2	Georgia	25
3	Maryland	25
4	Missouri	25
5	North Carolina	25
6	Utah	25
7	**Virginia**	**25**
8	**Minnesota**	**24.90909091**
9	**Florida**	**24.72727273**
10	Iowa	24.45454545
11	**Indiana**	**24.27272727**
12	South Carolina	24.27272727
13	Nebraska	24.18181818
14	Kansas	24
15	New Mexico	24
16	Ohio	24
17	Vermont	24
18	Washington	23.81818182
19	Tennessee	23.63636364
20	Wyoming	23.63636364
21	Alaska	23.6
22	Nevada	23.45454545

23	Oklahoma	23.45454545
24	Texas	23.36363636
25	South Dakota	23.28571429
26	Idaho	23.18181818
27	New Hampshire	23.09090909
28	Alabama	23
29	Arkansas	23
30	Connecticut	23
31	Maine	23
32	Mississippi	23
33	New York	23
34	Pennsylvania	23
35	North Dakota	22.90909091
36	**Massachusetts**	**22.81818182**
37	Michigan	22.81818182
38	Oregon	22.81818182
39	New Jersey	22.72727273
40	Rhode Island	22.72727273
41	**Colorado**	**22.54545455**
42	Hawaii	22.54545455
43	Arizona	22.45454545
44	Montana	22.45454545
45	Wisconsin	22.45454545
46	West Virginia	22.36363636
47	**Illinois**	**22.27272727**
48	Kentucky	22
49	**Louisiana**	**21.18181818**
50	California	19.72727273

Note: States in which I conducted interviews are in bold.

Appendix B: State Rankings on Two Indicators of Size of Government

State and Local Full-Time Equivalent Employees (FTE) per 1,000 State Population (2011)

Rank	State	FTE
1	Nevada	41.97336929
2	Arizona	43.31581696
3	Michigan	46.23018985
4	Pennsylvania	46.45148674
5	California	46.48397778
6	**Florida**	**46.60406888**
7	Rhode Island	47.31846796
8	**Massachusetts**	**48.68861438**
9	**Illinois**	**48.71462276**
10	Idaho	49.57081613
11	Wisconsin	49.64628284
12	**Indiana**	**50.56113914**
13	Washington	50.71230936
14	Oregon	50.95717587
15	Tennessee	51.13836454
16	Ohio	51.51126237
17	Connecticut	51.72411386
18	**Minnesota**	**51.85897257**
19	Georgia	51.88640895
20	Utah	52.38884263
21	Maryland	52.67943988
22	Missouri	52.7909617
23	**Colorado**	**52.79983802**
24	Hawaii	53.584859
25	South Carolina	54.19139474
26	**Virginia**	**54.20013131**
27	New Hampshire	54.82728642
28	Delaware	54.84409707
29	New Jersey	55.33447717
30	South Dakota	55.6388806
31	West Virginia	55.89253645
32	Texas	56.48358396
33	Kentucky	56.49779968
34	Oklahoma	56.64157902
35	Maine	56.74648468

36	North Carolina	57.58511893
37	Iowa	57.88703883
38	Montana	57.97841913
39	Alabama	59.29490249
40	New Mexico	60.35085562
41	New York	60.39913185
42	**Louisiana**	**61.55346334**
43	Vermont	63.29348324
44	Mississippi	64.46003911
45	Arkansas	64.53688062
46	Nebraska	65.65250638
47	North Dakota	65.86473509
48	Kansas	68.55823168
49	Alaska	75.74600328
50	Wyoming	92.81221069

Note: States in which I conducted interviews are in bold.

State and Local Payroll (by $1,000) per 1,000 State Population (2011)

Rank	State	Payroll
1	Tennessee	2,050.85
2	Idaho	2,077.46
3	Arizona	2,100.18
4	**Florida**	**2,172.27**
5	Maine	2,173.22
6	South Dakota	2,188.27
7	Georgia	2,190.36
8	Missouri	2,197.76
9	**Indiana**	**2,213.09**
10	Kentucky	2,223.31
11	West Virginia	2,223.42
12	Oklahoma	2,235.38
13	South Carolina	2,272.36
14	Utah	2,311.65
15	Arkansas	2,389.26
16	Nevada	2,399.76
17	Pennsylvania	2,411.23
18	Mississippi	2,442.51
19	North Carolina	2,470.75
20	Alabama	2,477.42
21	Montana	2,508.15
22	Michigan	2,515.96
23	Wisconsin	2,537.01
24	New Hampshire	2,537.51

(*continued on the next page*)

Rank	State	Payroll
25	Texas	2,542.99
26	**Virginia**	**2,548.88**
27	Ohio	2,568.27
28	New Mexico	2,574.37
29	Louisiana	2,623.52
30	Hawaii	2,679.94
31	Oregon	2,688.67
32	**Illinois**	**2,731.75**
33	**Colorado**	**2,736.71**
34	Delaware	2,773.27
35	**Minnesota**	**2,805.80**
36	**Massachusetts**	**2,841.22**
37	Rhode Island	2,851.23
38	Iowa	2,862.93
39	Kansas	2,872.21
40	North Dakota	2,934.52
41	Vermont	2,991.04
42	Nebraska	3,021.70
43	Maryland	3,081.37
44	Washington	3,138.40
45	California	3,138.80
46	Connecticut	3,229.66
47	New Jersey	3,607.12
48	New York	3,877.23
49	Wyoming	4,422.56
50	Alaska	4,573.12

Note: States in which I conducted interviews are in bold.

Appendix C: State Rankings on Two Measures of Political Culture or Partisanship

Average Ranney Index from 1975 to 2004

Rank	State	Average Ranney Index[a]
1	Idaho	0.2723667
2	South Dakota	0.28405
3	Utah	0.3102417
4	Wyoming	0.3216417
5	New Hampshire	0.3514
6	Kansas	0.361775
7	Arizona	0.3787167
8	North Dakota	0.38035
9	Nebraska	0.3937333
10	**Colorado**	**0.3958083**
11	Pennsylvania	0.4196
12	**Indiana**	**0.4267917**
13	Montana	0.442475
14	Ohio	0.44365
15	Alaska	0.448275
16	New York	0.4836667
17	Michigan	0.4852083
18	Iowa	0.4973917
19	Vermont	0.5212167
20	New Jersey	0.5241667
21	Delaware	0.537
22	**Illinois**	**0.5381833**
23	Nevada	0.5429083
24	Oregon	0.5579333
25	Wisconsin	0.5591833
26	Maine	0.5740167
27	**Minnesota**	**0.5833333**
28	Washington	0.5899
29	**Florida**	**0.5914333**
30	Connecticut	0.5994833
31	**Virginia**	**0.6113**
32	Tennessee	0.6178667
33	Missouri	0.6238

(*continued on the next page*)

Rank	State	Average Ranney Index[a]
34	Texas	0.628825
35	South Carolina	0.6497667
36	New Mexico	0.6517417
37	California	0.6564417
38	Oklahoma	0.6816917
39	North Carolina	0.695625
40	Kentucky	0.7235917
41	Massachusetts	0.7237333
42	Maryland	0.7323083
43	Georgia	0.7378083
44	Rhode Island	0.7423167
45	West Virginia	0.74455
46	**Louisiana**	**0.7466333**
47	Hawaii	0.7582583
48	Arkansas	0.7756667
49	Mississippi	0.7866583
50	Alabama	0.7917833

Note: States in which I conducted interviews are in bold.

[a]Austin Ranney, "Parties in State Politics," *Politics in the American States: A Comparative Analysis* (Boston: Little, Brown, 1971).

State Political Culture

Rank	State	Political Culture[a]
1	**Minnesota**	**1**
2	Washington	1.66
3	**Colorado**	**1.8**
4	Iowa	2
5	Michigan	2
6	North Dakota	2
7	Oregon	2
8	Utah	2
9	Wisconsin	2
10	Maine	2.33
11	New Hampshire	2.33
12	Vermont	2.33
13	Idaho	2.5
14	Connecticut	3
15	Montana	3
16	Rhode Island	3
17	South Dakota	3
18	California	3.55
19	New York	3.62

20	Kansas	3.66
21	**Massachusetts**	**3.66**
22	Nebraska	3.66
23	New Jersey	4
24	Wyoming	4
25	Pennsylvania	4.28
26	**Illinois**	**4.72**
27	Nevada	5
28	Ohio	5.16
29	Arizona	5.66
30	Alaska	6
31	**Indiana**	**6.33**
32	Delaware	7
33	Maryland	7
34	New Mexico	7
35	Texas	7.11
36	West Virginia	7.33
37	Kentucky	7.4
38	Missouri	7.66
39	**Florida**	**7.8**
40	**Virginia**	**7.86**
41	**Louisiana**	**8**
42	Hawaii	8.25
43	Oklahoma	8.25
44	North Carolina	8.5
45	Tennessee	8.5
46	Alabama	8.57
47	South Carolina	8.75
48	Georgia	8.8
49	Arkansas	9
50	Mississippi	9

Note: States in which I conducted interviews are in bold.

[a]Ira Sharkansky, "The Utility of Elazar's Political Culture: A Research Note," *Polity* 2, no. 1 (1969): 66–83; John R. Baker, "Exploring the 'Missing Link': Political Culture as an Explanation of the Occupational Status and Diversity of State Legislators in Thirty States," *Western Political Quarterly* 43, no. 3 (1990): 597–611.

Appendix D: Diagnostics for the Event History Analysis and Cox Proportional Hazards Model

The event history analysis (EHA) model used here is:

Rate of OIG adoption
= f (convictions, state investment, partisan competition, percent of neighbors, federal OIGs)

To perform the EHA, I used a Cox Proportional Hazards model, which is a statistical approach that requires neither parametric statistics nor a normal distribution of time to event (i.e., the number of years until the adoption of an

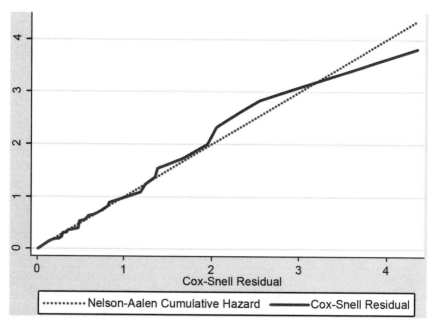

Figure A.1. Line Chart Comparing the Cox-Snell Residual with the Nelson-Aalen Cumulative Hazard

OIG in a state). The model is also amenable to discrete periods of time, as is used here, each year being the period of time in question.

As a preliminary step to test the appropriateness of this model, I checked potential multicollinearity in the model. As recommended by Paul Allison,[1] I used a linear regression with time until OIG adoption as the dependent variable, because the Cox regression does not provide collinearity diagnostics. This diagnostic demonstrates that the variance inflation factors for each of the independent variables ranges from 1.13 to 2, well below 10, the level at which multicollinearity is a problem.

A second step before running the model for purposes of interpretation is to examine whether any of the variables violate the assumption of proportionality of hazards, which is required for the Cox model. Comparing the full model with a model made up of time-dependent variables, I found that none of the variables violated this assumption at $p < 0.01$. No other variable diagnostics were required.

The final model, which has an overall p value of 0.0000, has a fairly good result to a goodness of fit test, comparing Cox-Snell residuals with the Nelson-Aalen cumulative hazard, as shown in figure A.1.

NOTES

CHAPTER 1. THE IDEA OF AN OFFICE OF INSPECTOR GENERAL

1. The New York City Department of Investigation is counted only once, although it is an umbrella agency that includes over fifty inspectors general who oversee city agencies.

2. See, for example, Paul C. Light, *Monitoring Government: Inspectors General and the Search for Accountability* (Washington, DC: Brookings Institution Press, 2011); Kathryn E. Newcomer, "Opportunities and Incentives for Improving Program Quality: Auditing and Evaluating," *Public Administration Review* 54, no. 2 (1994): 147–154; Kathryn E. Newcomer, "The Changing Nature of Accountability: The Role of the Inspector General in Federal Agencies," *Public Administration Review* 58, no. 2 (1998): 129–136; Kathryn E. Newcomer and George Grob, "Federal Offices of the Inspector General: Thriving on Chaos?" *The American Review of Public Administration* 34, no. 3 (2004): 235–251; Carmen R. Apaza, *Integrity and Accountability in Government: Homeland Security and the Inspector General* (New York: Routledge, 2016); Charles A. Johnson, Kathryn E. Newcomer, and Angela Allison, *Balancing Independence and Positive Engagement: How Inspectors General Work with Agencies and Congress* (Washington, DC: IBM Center for the Business of Government, 2015); Nadia Hilliard, *The Accountability State: US Federal Inspectors General and the Pursuit of Democratic Integrity* (Lawrence: University Press of Kansas, 2017).

3. Congress divided HEW into the Department of Education and Department of Health and Human Services in 1979.

4. This agency no longer exists. Its responsibilities are now handled by the United States Agency for International Development (USAID).

5. Light, *Monitoring Government*.

6. Light, *Monitoring Government*.

7. Representatives from four federal agencies, all in the field of intelligence, declined to provide the year that their OIG was created.

8. Light, *Monitoring Government*.

9. Newcomer, "Opportunities and Incentives"; Newcomer and Grob, "Federal Offices of the Inspector General."

10. Apaza, *Integrity and Accountability*; Hilliard, *The Accountability State*.

11. Johnson et al., *Balancing Independence*.

12. Data on the dates of creation were not available for seven OIGs. The three multijurisdictional OIGs are also not included in this graph.

13. Mark Bovens, "Analysing and Assessing Accountability: A Conceptual Framework 1," *European Law Journal* 13, no. 4 (2007): 447–468.

14. For an alternative take, see Deborah A. Stone, *Policy Paradox and Political Reason* (Glenview, IL: Scott Foresman, 1988).

15. Herman Finer, "Better Government Personnel," *Political Science Quarterly* 51, no. 4 (1936): 569–599; Finer, "Administrative Responsibility in Democratic Government," *Public* (1941): 335–350; Carl J. Friedrich, "Public Policy and the Nature of Administrative Responsibility," *Public* (1940): 3–24.

16. Hilliard, *The Accountability State.*

17. Finer, "Better Government Personnel"; Finer, "Administrative Responsibility."

18. Friedrich, "Public Policy."

19. Barbara S. Romzek and Melvin J. Dubnick, "Accountability in the Public Sector: Lessons from the Challenger Tragedy," *Public Administration Review* 47, no. 3 (1987): 227–238.

20. Jonathan G. S. Koppell, "Pathologies of Accountability: ICANN and the Challenge of "Multiple Accountabilities Disorder," *Public Administration Review* 65, no. 1 (2005): 94–108.

21. Melvin J. Dubnick and Justin O'Brien, "Rethinking the Obsession: Accountability and the Financial Crisis," in *Accountable Governance: Problems and Promises*, eds. Melvin J. Dubnick and H. George Frederickson (Abingdon, UK: Routledge, 2011), 282–301.

22. United States Military Academy, "History of the U.S. Army Inspector General," (n.d.), accessed June 21, 2019, https://westpoint.edu/about/west-point-staff/inspector-general/history.

23. Light, *Monitoring Government.*

24. Philip Selznick, *Leadership in Administration: A Sociological Interpretation* (New Orleans, LA: Quid Pro Books, 2011).

25. Lauren B. Edelman, Christopher Uggen, and Howard S. Erlanger, "The Endogeneity of Legal Regulation: Grievance Procedures as Rational Myth," *American Journal of Sociology* 105, no. 2 (1999): 406–454; W. Richard Scott, "The Adolescence of Institutional Theory," *Administrative Science Quarterly* 32, no. 4 (1987): 493–511; W. Richard Scott, "Institutions and Organizations: Toward a Theoretical Synthesis," *Institutional Environments and Organizations: Structural Complexity and Individualism* (Thousand Oaks, CA: Sage, 1994), 55–80; Paul J. DiMaggio and Walter W. Powell, "The Iron Cage Revisited: Institutional Isomorphism and Collective Rationality in Organizational Fields," *American Sociological Review* 48, no. 2 (1983): 147–160.

26. John W. Meyer and Brian Rowan, "Institutionalized Organizations: Formal Structure as Myth and Ceremony," *American Journal of Sociology* 83, no. 2 (1977): 340–363.

27. Light, *Monitoring Government.*

28. Inspector General Act of 1978, as amended, 5 U.S.C. Appendix §3 (2010).

29. IG Act of 1978, as amended, §3.

30. IG Act of 1978, as amended, §6.

31. Confidential personal communication, 2013.

32. Palm Beach County, Florida, Office of Inspector General Ordinance, Ordinance No. 2009-049 §2-423.4 (2009).

33. Palm Beach County, Ordinance No. 2009-049 §2-423.4.

34. IG Act of 1978, as amended, §3.

35. Palm Beach County, Ordinance No. 2009-049 §2-430.

36. IG Act of 1978, as amended, §6.

37. IG Act of 1978, as amended, §6.

38. Massachusetts Office of the Inspector General Act of 1980, Ann. Laws Mass., Gen. Laws ch. 12A §15 (2009).

39. Virginia Office of the State Inspector General Act, Va. Code Ann. §2.2–307, et seq. §2.2-311 (2013).

40. Melvin J. Dubnick and H. George Frederickson, "Public Accountability: Performance Measurement, the Extended State, and the Search for Trust," Washington DC: National Academy of Public Administration & The Kettering Foundation (2011); Bovens, "Analysing and Assessing Accountability."

41. It should be emphasized that OIGs are not the only units at the state and local levels that perform oversight akin to that provided by OIGs. Units such as legislative auditors or city auditors perform similar functions. Thus, it should not be concluded that states and cities without OIGs lack all monitoring. Nevertheless, the focus of this research is the increasing spread of the OIG concept and a state or city's deliberate choice to create an OIG or rename its oversight unit with the title "Inspector General."

42. James G. March and Johan P. Olsen, *Democratic Governance* (New York, NY: Free Press, 1995).

43. Light, *Monitoring Government.*

CHAPTER 2. PHASE I: CONCEPTUALIZATION

1. John W. Kingdon and James A. Thurber, *Agendas, Alternatives, and Public Policies*, vol. 45 (Boston: Little, Brown, 1984).

2. Kingdon and Thurber, *Agendas, Alternatives*, 3

3. James G. March and Johan P. Olsen, *Rediscovering Institutions* (New York, NY: Simon and Schuster, 2010); James G. March and Johan P. Olsen, *Democratic Governance* (New York, NY: Free Press, 1995).

4. Kingdon and Thurber, *Agendas, Alternatives.*

5. Kingdon and Thurber, *Agendas, Alternatives.*

6. An act creating a state inspector general, Connecticut H.R. Res. 5090, 9806–9807 (May 29, 1985).

7. Kingdon and Thurber, *Agendas, Alternatives.*

8. Kingdon and Thurber, *Agendas, Alternatives.*

9. Personal communication #7, June 18, 2012; personal communication #16, July 24, 2013; personal communication #17, July 24, 2013; personal communication #19, July 25,

2013; personal communication #25, July 26, 2013; personal communication #26, July 30, 2013; personal communication #35, November 5, 2013; personal communication #36, November 6, 2013; personal communication #38, November 7, 2013.

10. Massachusetts Office of Inspector General, "Inspector General of Massachusetts," webpage, 2014, accessed July 1, 2019, http://www.mass.gov/ig/.

11. Massachusetts Office of the Inspector General Act of 1980, Ann. Laws Mass., GL ch. 12A (2013).

12. Massachusetts Special Commission Concerning State and County Buildings, "Final Report to the Massachusetts General Court of the Special Commission Concerning State and County Buildings," vol. 1 (Boston: The Commission, 1980).

13. Massachusetts Special Commission Concerning State and County Buildings.

14. Massachusetts Office of Inspector General, webpage.

15. Massachusetts Special Commission Concerning State and County Buildings.

16. Massachusetts Special Commission Concerning State and County Buildings.

17. Massachusetts Special Commission Concerning State and County Buildings.

18. Massachusetts Special Commission Concerning State and County Buildings.

19. Massachusetts Special Commission Concerning State and County Buildings.

20. Massachusetts Special Commission Concerning State and County Buildings.

21. Massachusetts Special Commission Concerning State and County Buildings.

22. Massachusetts Special Commission Concerning State and County Buildings.

23. Larry Baldacci, "3-Year Record of Disaster in Making-Documents Trace the Tragedy of Slain 3-Year-Old," *Chicago Sun-Times*, May 3, 1993.

24. Cameron McWhirter and Andrew Gottesman, "Good Luck to You, Mother," *Chicago Tribune*, May 9, 1993.

25. McWhirter and Gottesman, "Good Luck."

26. McWhirter and Gottesman, "Good Luck."

27. McWhirter and Gottesman, "Good Luck"; "Justice and Amanda Wallace," *Chicago Tribune*, June 22, 1996.

28. R. Bruce Dold, "No Child Deserves This Boy's Pitiful Life," *Chicago Tribune*, May 24, 1996.

29. See, e.g., Diane BuGay, "Ounce of Prevention," *Chicago Tribune*, June 6, 1993; Carol D. Leonnig, "Probe: DHS Watchdog Cozy with Officials, Altered Reports as He Sought Top Job," *Washington Post*, April 24, 2014; K. Longmire, "How Long Must Children Pay the Price?" *Chicago Sun-Times*, May 23, 1993; E. Millard, "Stop Finger-Pointing over Child's Death," *Chicago Sun-Times*, May 21, 1993; Seiichi Michael Yasutake, "Sensitive Treatment," *Chicago Tribune*, August 17, 1997.

30. See, e.g., Larry Baldacci, "Edgar Sets up an Overseer for DCFS Personnel," *Chicago Sun-Times*, April 30, 1993; "The System Is the Scapegoat," *Chicago Tribune*, October 29, 1993; "What Went Wrong in the Courtroom," *Chicago Tribune*, May 2, 1993; "Lynching of Joseph: Suddenly the State Decides It Gives a Damn about Tortured Kids," *Journal Star*, May 16, 1993; Ricard Roeper, "Is It Ever Proper to Take Someone's Birth Right?" *Chicago Sun-Times*, May 3, 1993; "3-Year-Old Joseph's Death Was a Tragedy of Errors," editorial, *State Journal-Register*, May 10, 1993; "What about

Joshua?" *Chicago Tribune*, April 20, 1994; "Victimization of Joshua Wallace," *Chicago Tribune*, May 17, 1995; R. Bruce Dold, "No Child Deserves This Boy's Pitiful Life," *Chicago Tribune*, May 24, 1996; "Peace Comes to Amanda Wallace," *Chicago Tribune*, August 5, 1997.

31. "In Memory of Joseph Wallace," *Chicago Tribune*, April 21, 1993.

32. Larry Baldacci, "Edgar Sets Up an Overseer for DCFS Personnel," *Chicago Sun-Times*, April 30, 1993.

33. Baldacci, "Edgar Sets Up."

34. Kingdon and Thurber, *Agendas, Alternatives.*

35. The survey data do not tell us if these agency leaders support the concept of an OIG to oversee their own agency's activities because they initially view an OIG as a toothless form of oversight that they can control or that they view the model as actually helpful to them, perhaps by offering investigations or ideas that they themselves could not. Themes of pushback against OIGs described in chapters 3 and 4 suggest the former is more common.

36. Graeme Boushey, *Policy Diffusion Dynamics in America* (Cambridge, UK: Cambridge University Press, 2010).

37. See, e.g., Andrew Karch, *Democratic Laboratories: Policy Diffusion among the American States* (Ann Arbor, MI: University of Michigan Press, 2007).

38. Personal communication #5, May 18, 2012; personal communication #9, July 3, 2013; personal communication #12, July 22, 2013; personal communication #15, July 24, 2013; personal communication #20, July 25, 2013; personal communication #23, July 26, 2013; personal communication #29, October 10, 2013; personal communication #33, October 17, 2013.

39. Personal communication #8, May 29, 2013; personal communication #18, July 25, 2013; personal communication #28, July 31, 2013; personal communication #37, November 6, 2013; personal communication #39, November 7, 2013.

40. Minnesota Department of Human Services, "DHS announces creation of the Office of Inspector General," August 18, 2011, http://www.dhs.state.mn.us/main/idcplg?Idc Service=GET_DYNAMIC_CONVERSION&dID=119547.

41. Minnesota Department of Human Services, "DHS Announces."

42. Minnesota Department of Human Services, "DHS Announces," para. 1.

43. Bob Clift, "Capture the Synergy," *Florida Department of Transportation Office of Inspector General Examiner*, 2014, accessed July 7, 2019, http://fdotoig.wordpress.com/2014/03/03/capture-the-synergy/.

44. Florida Inspector General Act of 1994, *Florida* Stat. § 20.055 (2013).

45. Purdue University, Office of the President, "Mitchell E. Daniels, Jr. Biography," personal biography, 2019, accessed July 1, 2019, https://www.purdue.edu/president/about/biography.php.

46. L. Morris, "On the Road to Reform—Gov.-Elect Daniels Realized the State Needs Not Just Mechanisms, but the Right Attitude," *Fort Wayne (IN) News-Sentinel*, 4A, December 28, 2004; "Inspector General," editorial, *Evansville Courier & Press*, March 20, 2005; Niki Kelly, "Capital Changes: Inspector General Begins Fight on

Fraud," *Fort Wayne (IN) Journal Gazette*, July 4, 2005; Indiana Executive Order No. 05-03 (2005); Indiana Inspector General Act of 2005, Burns Ind. Code Ann. § 4-2-7 (2013).

47. J. Merriner and L. Rotenberk, "Daley Asks Anti-Corruption Office," *Chicago Sun-Times*, January 31, 1989.

48. Thomas Hardy, "Sawyer, Daley Take Spotlight in Mayor's Race," *Chicago Tribune*, January 8, 1989.

49. William E. Schmidt, "Man in the News; Chicago Mayor from a New Mold; Richard Michael Daley," *New York Times*, April 5, 1989.

50. Chicago, Illinois, Office of Inspector General City Ordinance, ch. 2–56 (1989).

51. Susan Saulny, "Portrait of a Politician: Vengeful and Profane," *New York Times*, December 10, 2008; Annie Sweeney, "Feds Seek 15-, 20-Year Sentence for Blagojevich," *Chicago Tribune*, December 1, 2011.

52. Saulny, "Portrait of a Politician"; Sweeney, "Feds Seek."

53. "Events leading to Ryan's indictment," *Chicago Tribune*, accessed July 1, 2019, https://www.chicagotribune.com/news/breaking/chi-031218ryanevents-graphic-graphic.html.

54. Illinois Executive Order No. 3 (2003).

55. Illinois Executive Ethics Commission and Executive Inspectors General Act of 2006, Il. 5 ILCS 430/20 (2013).

56. "Reformers Hope Ryan Indictments Resurrect Ethics Legislation," *Journal Gazette*, April 8, 2002; "Past Problems with Inspectors General Cloud Blagojevich Ethics Plan," *Journal Gazette*, November 3, 2003.

57. *Colorado Senate Judiciary Committee: Hearing on HB 1317, Concerning the Clarification of the Responsibilities of Investigative Positions within the Department of Corrections*, April 5, 1999.

58. Confidential personal communication, 2013.

59. Confidential personal communication, 2013.

60. *Colorado Senate Judiciary Committee.*

61. Colorado Legislative Council Staff, "Digest of Bills Enacted by the Sixty-Second General Assembly," H.B. 99-1317, Department of Corrections, Executive Director, Appointment of Inspector General and Investigators, June 1999, pp. 26–27.

62. *Colorado Senate Judiciary Committee.*

63. Colorado Legislative Council Staff, "Digest of Bills."

64. Confidential personal communication, 2013.

65. Confidential personal communication, 2013.

66. Richmond, Virginia, Inspector General Function, Div. 7, § 2-230, et seq. (2008).

67. Confidential personal communication, 2013.

68. Clerk of the Circuit Court of Pinellas County, Florida, Division of Inspector General, Division of the Inspector General, webpage, 2019, accessed July 1, 2019, https://www.mypinellasclerk.org/Home/Inspector-General#599114-about-the-ig.

69. Kingdon and Thurber, *Agendas, Alternatives.*

70. Kingdon and Thurber, *Agendas, Alternatives.*

71. Melvin J. Dubnick and Justin O'Brien, "Rethinking the Obsession: Accountabil-

ity and the Financial Crisis," in Melvin J. Dubnick and H. George Frederickson, eds., *Accountable Governance: Problems and Promises* (New York, NY: Routledge, 2014).

72. Personal communication #27, July 31, 2013.

73. Karch, *Democratic Laboratories*; Kingdon and Thurber, *Agendas, Alternatives*.

74. L. Ortiz, "Phelan Unsure of Need for Inspector Job," *Chicago Sun-Times*, April 8, 1993.

75. Ortiz, "Phelan unsure."

76. Steve Patterson, "New County Fraud-Fighter Wants to Beef up Staff," *Chicago Sun-Times*, May 26, 2004.

77. Abdon M. Pallasch, "County Board Oks Hiring Watchdog: Commissioners Vote to Settle Shakman Suit," *Chicago Sun-Times*, November 30, 2006.

78. Natasha Korecki, "2 Parties Back Proposal for Toll Authority Inspector," *Arlington Heights (IL) Daily Herald*, January 31, 1997.

79. Korecki, "2 Parties."

80. Associated Press, "Blagojevich Proposes Changes to Head off Toll Increases," *The Mattoon (IL) Journal Gazette*, November 15, 2002.

81. "Sabotaging Tollway Reform," *Beacon News*, September 4, 2003.

82. Confidential personal communication, 2013; Illinois Toll Highway Inspector General, Il. 605 ILCS 10/8.5 (2013).

83. Minn. HF 3047 (2010); Minn. HF 2256 (2010); Minn. HF 4049 (2008); Minn. HF 4119 (2008).

84. Confidential personal communication, 2013.

85. Minnesota Child Care Provider and Recipient Fraud Investigations, Minn. Stat. § 245E.01 (2013).

86. Personal communication #9; personal communication #25; personal communication #27; personal communication #28; personal communication #29; personal communication #37, 2013; personal communication #38; personal communication #39.

87. Personal communication, #28.

88. Personal communication #39.

89. Personal communication #25.

90. Personal communication #27.

91. Personal communication #9.

92. Personal communication #29.

93. Personal communication #38.

94. Personal communication #23; "Future of Ethics Reform in the Hands of the Governor," *Mattoon (IL) Journal Gazette*, June 9, 2003; Richard Roeper, "Power-Grabbing Governor Soon Will See Error of His Ways-Blagojevich Wants to Set Up a Super Inspector General," *Chicago Sun-Times*, June 21, 2003.

95. Personal communication #17; personal communication #18.

96. "Future of Ethics"; Roeper, "Power-Grabbing."

97. Frances Stokes Berry and William D. Berry, "State Lottery Adoptions as Policy Innovations: An Event History Analysis," *American Political Science Review* 84, no. 2 (1990): 395–415.

98. Local OIG adoptions are not included in this analysis because comparable data about local conditions are not available.

99. Box-Steffensmeier, Janet M., Janet M. Box-Steffensmeier, and Bradford S. Jones, *Event History Modeling: A Guide for Social Scientists* (Cambridge, UK: Cambridge University Press, 2004).

100. See, e.g., Berry and Berry, "State Lottery Adoptions."

101. Lawrence B. Mohr, "Determinants of Innovation in Organizations," *American Political Science Review* 63, no. 1 (1969): 111–126; Berry and Berry, "State Lottery Adoptions."

102. Karch, *Democratic Laboratories*.

103. Sanford C. Gordon, "Assessing Partisan Bias in Federal Public Corruption Prosecutions," *American Political Science Review* 103, no. 4 (2009): 534–554; Richard T. Boylan and Cheryl X. Long, "Measuring Public Corruption in the American States: A Survey of State House Reporters," *State Politics & Policy Quarterly* 3, no. 4 (2003): 420–438.

104. Dick Simpson, James Nowlan, Thomas J. Gradel, Melissa Mouritsen Zmuda, David Sterrett, and Douglas Cantor, "Chicago and Illinois, Leading the Pack in Corruption," (Chicago: University of Illinois at Chicago, Department of Political Science and Institute for Government and Public Affairs, 2012), http://www.uic.edu/depts /pols/ChicagoPolitics/leadingthepack.pdf.

105. Graeme Boushey (*Policy Diffusion Dynamics*) suggests that things such as salaries of legislators, numbers of days in session, and size of legislation staff are important predictors of innovation, because those states have legislators with the capacity to do more analysis than other states. Further, Boushey notes that capacity has a different impact on diffusion depending on the type of innovation. He finds that regulatory innovations are more likely to be adopted in states with greater capacity, whereas morality-based or governance-based innovations are more likely to be adopted in states with lower capacity. He attributes this to the fact that regulatory issues are more technically complex and require more study, as opposed to issues of morality or governance. Also, he notes that governance issues, such as term limits, are more likely to be adopted in states that have direct democracy mechanisms, such as initiatives or referendums. Nonetheless, legislative capacity may not be as applicable to OIG adoption as it might be for other policies. First, OIGs are not exclusively adopted by legislators. Sometimes it is the governor or an agency head who acts to adopt an OIG on the state level. Second, according to the survey, OIG adoption is rarely called for by the public. In order to capture capacity that is most relevant to OIG adoption, this research examines levels of a state's investment in its bureaucracy.

106. Although I have not included legislative capacity as a variable in this analysis, I include a measure of partisan control/partisan competition on the grounds that this variable is more comprehensive in that it includes consideration of partisan control of the governor's office in addition to the legislature, and governors may have direct influence over bureaucratic reorganization; Austin Ranney, "Parties in State Politics." In

Politics in the American States 3, Herbert Jacob and Kenneth Nelson Vines, eds. *Politics in the American States: A Comparative Analysis*. Little, Brown, 1965.

107. Ranney, "Parties in State Politics."

108. Carl Klarner, "Other Scholars' Competitiveness Measures," Harvard Dataverse, 2013, accessed July 2, 2019, https://doi.org/10.7910/dvn/qsdylh, Harvard Dataverse, V1, (2013) [July 2, 2019].

109. Ira Sharkansky, "The Utility of Elazar's Political Culture: A Research Note," *Polity* 2, no. 1 (1969): 66–83.

110. Robert D. Putnam, *Bowling Alone: The Collapse and Revival of American Community* (New York: Simon and Schuster, 2001).

111. R. S. Erikson, G. C. Wright, and J. P. McIver, "Public Opinion in the States: A Quarter Century of Change and Stability," in Jeffery E. Cohen, ed., *Public Opinion in State Politics* (Stanford, CA: Stanford University Press, 2006), 229–253.

112. Berry and Berry, "State Lottery Adoptions."

113. Charles R. Shipan, and Craig Volden, "Policy Diffusion: Seven Lessons for Scholars and Practitioners," *Public Administration Review* 72, no. 6 (2012): 788–796.

114. Berry and Berry, "State Lottery Adoptions."

115. Karch, *Democratic Laboratories*.

116. Boushey, *Policy Diffusion Dynamics*.

117. Karch, *Democratic Laboratories*; Boushey, *Policy Diffusion Dynamics*.

118. Personal communication #6, May 18, 2012; personal communication #32, October 17, 2013; personal communication #33; Minnesota Department of Human Services, "DHS Announces"; Massachusetts Special Commission Concerning State and County Buildings; An Act Creating a State Inspector General, Connecticut H.R. Res. 5090 (May 29, 1985).

119. M. Comlossy, "Fighting Medicaid Fraud," *State Legislatures Magazine*, 2013.

120. Confidential personal communication, 2013.

121. Minnesota Department of Human Services, "DHS Announces."

122. Kingdon and Thurber, *Agendas, Alternatives*.

123. Personal communication #20.

CHAPTER 3. PHASE II: DESIGN

1. See, e.g., Chicago, Illinois, Office of Inspector General City Ordinance, ch. 2–56 (1989); Florida Inspector General Act of 1994, *Florida* Stat. § 20.055 (2013); Illinois Executive Ethics Commission and Executive Inspectors General Act of 2006, 5 ILCS 430/20 (2013); Indiana Inspector General Act of 2005, Burns Ind. Code Ann. § 4-2-7 (2013).

2. See, e.g., Minnesota Department of Human Services, "DHS Announces Creation of the Office of Inspector General," August 18, 2011; personal communication #34, 2013; personal communication #36, 2013; personal communication #37, 2013.

3. E. M. Rogers, *Diffusion of Innovations*, 5th ed. (New York: Free Press, 2003); Frances Stokes Berry and William D. Berry, "State Lottery Adoptions as Policy Innovations: An Event History Analysis," *American Political Science Review* 84, no. 2 (1990): 395–415; Charles R. Epp, *Making Rights Real: Activists, Bureaucrats, and the Creation of the Legalistic State* (Chicago, IL: University of Chicago Press, 2010); Andrew Karch, *Democratic Laboratories: Policy Diffusion among the American States* (Ann Arbor, MI: University of Michigan Press, 2007); Dorothy M. Daley and James C. Garand, "Horizontal Diffusion, Vertical Diffusion, and Internal Pressure in State Environmental Policymaking, 1989–1998," *American Politics Research* 33, no. 5 (2005): 615–644; Graeme Boushey, *Policy Diffusion Dynamics in America* (Cambridge, UK: Cambridge University Press, 2010); Kyu-Nahm Jun and Christopher Weare, "Institutional Motivations in the Adoption of Innovations: The Case of E-Government," *Journal of Public Administration Research and Theory* 21, no. 3 (2010): 495–519.

4. Karch, *Democratic Laboratories*.

5. Association of Inspectors General, "Principles and Standards for Offices of Inspector General [Green Book]" (Philadelphia, PA: AIG, 2014), accessed July 9, 2019, http://inspectorsgeneral.org/files/2014/11/AIG-Principles-and-Standards-May-2014-Revision-2.pdf. Hereafter referred to as the Green Book.

6. Association of Inspectors General, "Model Legislation for the Establishment of Offices of Inspector General," 2002, accessed July 9, 2019, http://inspectorsgeneral.org/files/2011/01/IG-Model-Legislation.pdf.

7. Paul C. Light, *Monitoring Government: Inspectors General and the Search for Accountability* (Washington, DC: Brookings Institution Press, 2011).

8. Robert D. McFadden, "Billie Sol Estes, Texas Con Man Whose Fall Shook Up Washington, Dies at 88," *New York Times*, May 14, 2013.

9. Light, *Monitoring Government*.

10. "About" webpage of the Association of Inspectors General website, accessed June 30, 2014, www.inspectorsgeneral.org.

11. "About" webpage of the Association of Inspectors General website.

12. "Inspector General Institute" information page of the Association of Inspectors General website, 2019, accessed July 9, 2019, http://inspectorsgeneral.org/institutes/institute/.

13. Light, *Monitoring Government*, 33–34.

14. Association of Inspectors General, Green Book, 3.

15. Association of Inspectors General, Green Book, 3.

16. Personal communication #24, July 26, 2013.

17. Personal communication #24.

18. Personal communication #10, July 3, 2013.

19. Light, *Monitoring Government*.

20. Light, *Monitoring Government*.

21. Personal communication #29, October 10, 2013.

22. Light, *Monitoring Government*; Melvin J. Dubnick and H. George Frederickson,

Public Accountability: Performance Measurement, the Extended State, and the Search for Trust (Dayton, OH: Kettering Foundation, 2011).

23. Dubnick and Frederickson, *Public Accountability*, 8.

24. Association of Inspectors General, Green Book, 4; Association of Inspectors General, "Model Legislation," § 11.

25. Association of Inspectors General, Green Book, 4; Association of Inspectors General, "Model Legislation," § 11.

26. Association of Inspectors General, "Model Legislation," § 11.

27. Association of Inspectors General, "Model Legislation," § 11 (my emphasis).

28. Personal communication #29.

29. Personal communication #29.

30. Association of Inspectors General, "Model Legislation," § 12; Association of Inspectors General, Green Book; Association of Inspectors General, "Model Legislation," § 9.

31. Association of Inspectors General "Model Legislation," § 12; Association of Inspectors General, Green Book.

32. Association of Inspectors General, "Model Legislation," § 12; Association of Inspectors General, Green Book.

33. Association of Inspectors General, Green Book. See, e.g., Inspector General Act of 1978, 5 U.S.C. Appendix, as amended, § 6 (2010).

34. Association of Inspectors General, "Model Legislation," § 12; Association of Inspectors General, Green Book.

35. Association of Inspectors General, "Model Legislation," § 9; IG Act of 1978, as amended, § 7.

36. IG Act of 1978, as amended, § 6. A bill to grant such authority was introduced as recently as 2010 (H.R. 5815, 111th Cong.).

37. A 1991 bill that would have provided all OIGs blanket law-enforcement authority is discussed in Light, *Monitoring Government*, 189–194. Currently, only certain specified OIGs are exempt from needing to obtain the attorney general's approval of law-enforcement designation according to the IG Act of 1978, as amended, § 6.

38. Light, *Monitoring Government*, 23

39. Association of Inspectors General, Green Book, 8.

40. Association of Inspectors General, Green Book, 8–9.

41. Association of Inspectors General, Green Book, 9.

42. Association of Inspectors General, "Model Legislation," § 2 (my emphasis).

43. Association of Inspectors General, "Model Legislation," § 4.

44. Association of Inspectors General, "Model Legislation," § 5.

45. Association of Inspectors General, "Model Legislation," § 6.

46. Association of Inspectors General, "Model Legislation," § 4. In the federal system, hiring and firing protections are currently limited to three. First, IGs are selected on the basis of professional qualifications (IG Act of 1978, as amended, § 3). Second, IGs of large agencies are appointed by the president and confirmed by the Senate

(IG Act of 1978, as amended, § 3); however, (and thirdly) IGs with smaller regulatory boards are appointed by the boards (IG Act of 1978, as amended, § 8G). If removed from the position, the president is required to communicate reasons for removal to Congress in writing (IG Act of 1978, as amended, § 3).

47. Association of Inspectors General, "Model Legislation," § 7.

48. The budgets for federal OIGs are proposed by the IGs and aggregated by the president or agency head. Those OIGs whose IGs are appointed by the president have access to Congress to discuss their budgets and request increases. This independent relationship ensures that the agency cannot unilaterally retaliate against the OIG by cutting its budget if there is an audit or investigation that it does not like. See the IG Act of 1978, as amended, § 6; Project on Government Oversight, "Inspectors General: Many Lack Essential Tools for Independence," February 26, 2008, http://www.pogo.org/our-work/reports/2008/go-ig-20080226.html#Budget_Line_Items_and_Transparency. Those OIGs with IGs appointed by the agency head, usually regulatory boards, do not have the opportunity to discuss their budgets with Congress. They are dependent on their agencies to make their budget requests. Thus, "their budgets are dependent on the good will of their agency heads" to get their full requests (Project on Government Oversight, "Budget Line Items and Transparency," para. 2).

49. Association of Inspectors General, "Model Legislation," § 7.

50. Association of Inspectors General, "Model Legislation," § 8.

51. Association of Inspectors General, "Model Legislation," § 10.

52. Association of Inspectors General, "Model Legislation," § 10.

53. Association of Inspectors General, "Model Legislation." Federal OIGs are required to provide their prescribed semiannual reports. Any egregious and flagrant problems or abuses uncovered by the OIG are required to be reported to both Congress and the agency head (IG Act of 1978, as amended, § 5). Thus, an OIG has a secondary audience for its information and recommendations outside the agency it oversees.

54. Association of Inspectors General, "Model Legislation," § 4.

55. Massachusetts Special Commission Concerning State and County Buildings, "Final Report to the Massachusetts General Court of the Special Commission Concerning State and County Buildings," vol. 1 (Boston: The Commission, 1980). See https://archive.org/details/finalreporttogen13mass.

56. Massachusetts Office of the Inspector General Act of 1980, Ann. Laws Mass., GL ch. 12A (2013).

57. Massachusetts Office of the Inspector General Act of 1980 § 8.

58. Massachusetts Office of the Inspector General Act of 1980 § 7.

59. "Official Website" of the Massachusetts Office of the Inspector General, 2014, accessed July 7, 2019, http://www.mass.gov/ig/.

60. "Official Website" of the Massachusetts Office of the Inspector General.

61. See, e.g., Annotated Laws of Massachusetts, GL ch. 6A § 16V (2013).

62. Massachusetts Office of the Inspector General Act of 1980 § 9.

63. Massachusetts Office of the Inspector General Act of 1980 § 13.

64. Massachusetts Office of the Inspector General Act of 1980 § 9.

65. Massachusetts Office of the Inspector General Act of 1980 § 15.

66. Massachusetts Office of the Inspector General Act of 1980 § 11.

67. Massachusetts Office of the Inspector General Act of 1980 § 2.

68. Massachusetts Office of the Inspector General Act of 1980 § 2.

69. Massachusetts Office of the Inspector General Act of 1980 § 2.

70. Massachusetts Office of the Inspector General Act of 1980 § 4.

71. Massachusetts Office of the Inspector General Act of 1980 § 4.

72. Massachusetts Office of the Inspector General Act of 1980 § 12.

73. In 2013, the OIG did succeed in receiving a statutory reference to the OIG, which gives it a specific role in the Minnesota Child Care Provider and Recipient Fraud Investigations Act (2013), even though it lacks statutory creation. See the Minnesota Department of Human Services, "DHS Announces Creation of the Office of Inspector General," August 18, 2011, http://www.dhs.state.mn.us/main/idcplg?IdcService=GET_DYNAMIC_CONVERSION&dID=119547.

74. Minnesota Department of Human Services Office of Inspector General, "Office of Inspector General 2013 Session Overview," 2013, http://www.dhs.state.mn.us/main/groups/licensing/documents/pub/dhs16_177977.pdf.

75. Karch, *Democratic Laboratories*.

76. Minnesota Department of Human Services, "DHS announces."

77. Minnesota Department of Human Services, "DHS announces."

78. Kevin Featherly, "New DHS Inspector General Kerber Aims to Root Out Fraud, Client Abuse in Minnesota," *Legal Ledger*, November 16, 2011, http://politicsinminnesota.com/2011/11/new-dhs-inspector-general-kerber-aims-to-root-out-fraud-client-abuse/.

79. Featherly, "New DHS."

80. Confidential personal communication, 2013.

81. Featherly, "New DHS."

82. Confidential personal communication, 2013.

83. "Organization/management" webpage of the Minnesota Department of Human Services, accessed July 9, 2019, http://www.dhs.state.mn.us/main/idcplg?IdcService=GET_DYNAMIC_CONVERSION&RevisionSelectionMethod=LatestReleased&dDocName=id_000261.

84. Confidential personal communication, 2013.

85. Minnesota Department of Human Services Office of Inspector General, "Office of Inspector General."

86. Illinois Department of Human Services Act, 20 ILCS 1305/1–17 (2013).

87. Illinois Department of Human Services Act.

88. Illinois Department of Human Services Act.

89. Illinois Department of Human Services Act.

90. "History of OIG" webpage of the Illinois Department of Human Services Office of Inspector General, accessed July 9, 2019, http://www.dhs.state.il.us/page.aspx?item=29412.

91. M. Briggs, "Mental Patient Abuse Probe Set—Report Alleges Sex Attacks, Beatings," *Chicago Sun-Times*, September 8, 1986.

92. M. Lawrence, "State Acts on Patient Abuse—Mental Health Crackdown Today," *Chicago Sun-Times*, August 26, 1987.

93. Thomas Gerber, "Mental Home Abuse Probe Set—State Study Cites Faulty Reporting," *Chicago Sun-Times*, August 27, 1987.

94. Gerber, "Mental Home Abuse."

95. "History of OIG" webpage of the Illinois Department of Human Services Office of Inspector General, http://www.dhs.state.il.us/page.aspx?item=29412.

96. "History of OIG" webpage.

97. John F. Bibby and Thomas M. Holbrook, "Parties and Elections," in *Politics in the American States: A Comparative Analysis*, 8th ed., Virginia Gray, and Russell L. Hanson, eds. (Washington, DC: CQ Press, 2004), 62–99.

98. Massachusetts Special Commission Report.

99. Massachusetts Special Commission Report.

100. Massachusetts Special Commission Report.

101. Massachusetts Special Commission Report.

102. Massachusetts Special Commission Report.

103. Massachusetts Special Commission Report.

104. Massachusetts Special Commission Report.

105. Massachusetts Special Commission Report.

106. Massachusetts Office of the Inspector General Act of 1980, Ann. Laws Mass., GL ch. 12A § 10 (2013).

107. Massachusetts Office of Inspector General Act § 9.

108. J. Merriner and L. Rotenberk, "Daley Asks Anti-Corruption Office," *Chicago Sun-Times*, January 31, 1989.

109. "Chicago Is Ready for Reform," *Chicago Sun Times*, July 2, 1989.

110. "Council Fears Inspector General's Bite," *Chicago Tribune*, September 18, 1989; J. Kaplan, "Daley Inspector Denied a Key Power," *Chicago Tribune*, September 13, 1989.

111. Kaplan, "Daley Inspector."

112. Nick Bogert, "Chicago's New Inspector General a 'Watch Kitten'?," *Examiner*, 2010; Chicago, Illinois, Legislative Inspector General City Ordinance, ch. 2–55 (2013).

113. Bogert, "Chicago's New Inspector General"; "Thanks, Aldermen," editorial, *Chicago Tribune*, April 13, 2010, http://articles.chicagotribune.com/2010-04-13/opinion/ct-edit-inspector-20100413_1_aldermen-michael-shakman-inspector; Chicago, Illinois, Legislative Inspector General City Ordinance.

114. Chicago, Illinois, Legislative Inspector General City Ordinance.

115. Chicago, Illinois, Legislative Inspector General City Ordinance.

116. Chicago, Illinois, Legislative Inspector General City Ordinance.

117. Natasha Korecki, "Feds Seize Computers, Files on Chicago Officials from Outgoing Inspector General," *Politico*, November 16, 2015.

118. Florida Inspector General Act of 1994, *Florida* Stat. § 20.055 (2013).

119. Florida Inspector General Act of 1994.

120. Bob Clift, "Capture the Synergy," *Florida Department of Transportation Office of Inspector General Examiner*, 2014.

121. Confidential personal communication, 2013.

122. Final Bill Analysis, Florida H.R. Res. 1385 (2014).

123. Confidential personal communication, 2013.

124. Florida House of Representatives.

125. Florida House of Representatives.

126. Florida House of Representatives.

127. Colorado Revised Stat. (CSR) § 16-2.5-134 (2013).

128. Confidential personal communication, 2013.

129. "Office of the Inspector General" webpage of the Colorado Department of Corrections, accessed May 24, 2014, http://www.doc.state.co.us/office-inspector-general.

130. *Colorado Senate Judiciary Committee: Hearing on HB 1317, Concerning the Clarification of the Responsibilities of Investigative Positions within the Department of Corrections*, (April 5, 1999).

131. *Colorado Senate Judiciary Committee.*

132. Confidential personal communication, 2013.

133. Confidential personal communication, 2013.

134. Confidential personal communication, 2013.

135. "Office of the Inspector General" webpage of the Colorado Department of Corrections.

CHAPTER 4. PHASE III: IMPLEMENTATION

1. *Inspectors General: Independence, Access and Authority Hearing before the Committee on Oversight and Government Reform, House of Representatives*, 114th Cong., first session (February 3, 2015); Josh Hicks, "Dozens of Inspectors General Say Federal Agencies Hindering Oversight," *Washington Post*, August 6, 2014.

2. Paul C. Light, *Monitoring Government: Inspectors General and the Search for Accountability* (Washington, DC: Brookings Institution Press, 2011).

3. Graham T. Allison and Philip Zelikow, *Essence of Decision: Explaining the Cuban Missile Crisis*, first edition (Boston: Little, Brown, 1971); extended by Daniel P. Carpenter, *The Forging of Bureaucratic Autonomy: Reputations, Networks, and Policy Innovation in Executive Agencies, 1862–1928*, vol. 78. (Princeton, NJ: Princeton University Press, 2001).

4. Personal communication #18, July 25, 2013.

5. Personal communication #37, November 6, 2013.

6. It should be noted that this negative reaction to oversight is not unique to OIGs. A local IG who previously was the head of internal audit before the unit transitioned into an OIG stated: "This kind of fight [against our presence and our work]—we've always had it. It's not the change of the name or the title that caused it." Personal communication #37.

7. Cook County, Illinois, Office of the Independent Inspector General ordinance § 2-283 (2013).

8. Cook County, Inspector General ordinance.

9. Rob Olmstead, "Cook County Gets Closer to Having an Inspector General," *Arlington Heights (IL) Daily Herald*, June 27, 2008.

10. Steve Patterson, "Watchdog for County Corruption Ok'd—but Stroger Must Find Money for It," *Chicago Sun-Times*, July 25, 2007.

11. Steve Schmadeke, "Daley Nephew Vanecko Pleads Guilty in Koschman Death," *Chicago Tribune*, February 1, 2014.

12. Tim Novak and Chris Fusco, "State's Attorney Blocks Probe of Her Office— Who Killed David Koschman? A Watchdog's Investigation," *Chicago Sun-Times*, May 5, 2011.

13. Lisa Donovan, "Berrios Rejects Subpoena," *Chicago Sun-Times*, October 16, 2012.

14. Jon Seidel, "Cook County Inspector Taking Berrios to Court," *Chicago Sun-Times*, June 12, 2013.

15. Associated Press, Illinois State Wire, "Judge: Inspector Can Investigate Elective Offices," *Chicago Sun-Times*, January 16, 2014.

16. Confidential personal communication, 2013.

17. Confidential personal communication [emphasis added].

18. Confidential personal communication.

19. Confidential personal communication.

20. Confidential personal communication.

21. Confidential personal communication.

22. Confidential personal communication.

23. Confidential personal communication.

24. *Ferguson v. Patton*, 985 N.E.2d 1000 (Dec. 14, 2013); *Kendig v. Kendig*, 981 N.Y.S. 2d 411, App. Div. (2014).

25. Chicago, Illinois, Office of the Inspector General City Ordinance § 2-56-090 (1989).

26. *Ferguson v. Patton*.

27. *Ferguson v. Patton*.

28. *Ferguson v. Patton*.

29. Personal communication #32, October 17, 2013.

30. Massachusetts Special Commission Concerning State and County Buildings, "Final Report to the Massachusetts General Court of the Special Commission Concerning State and County Buildings," vol. 1 (Boston: The Commission, 1980).

31. Massachusetts Office of the Inspector General Act of 1980, Ann. Laws Mass., GL ch. 12A § 2 (2013).

32. Rob Olmstead, "Frustrated Official Seeks to Jumpstart Search Process," *Arlington Heights (IL) Daily Herald*, March 16, 2008.

33. Cook County, Illinois, Office of the Independent Inspector General Ordinance § 2-282 (2013).

34. Olmstead, "Frustrated Official."

35. Association of Inspectors General Training Conference, New Orleans, Louisiana, fall 2013.

36. K. Tarrant, "Random Musings: A Tale of Two I.G.'s and Other Contemplations," *Examiner*, 2013.

37. See, e.g., Frank Phillips, "Weld Stripping Watchdogs Of Bite, Critics Say," *Boston Globe*, April 2, 1991.

38. See, e.g., D. S. Wong and Don Aucoin, "House OK's 31.5% Raise for Inspector General," *Boston Globe*, April 16, 1997.

39. Melinda Deslatte, "Inspector General Asks Senators to Keep His Office," Associated Press, May 17, 2012; The Association of Inspectors General Training Conference, Clearwater Beach, Florida, fall 2012; The Association of Inspectors General Training Conference, 2013.

40. Association of Inspectors General Training Conference, 2013; Associated Press, Louisiana State Wire, "Notes and Quotes from the Louisiana Legislature," May 7, 2012; Barry Erwin, "So Why Is It Louisiana Doesn't Need An Inspector General?" Council for a Better Louisiana, May 25, 2012.

41. New Orleans, Louisiana, Office of the Inspector General, "OIG: New Orleans Office of Inspector General," (2014), accessed July 11, 2019, http://www.nolaoig.gov /about/mission-history.

42. Association of Inspectors General Training Conference, 2013.

43. Confidential personal communication, 2012.

44. R. Rhoden, "New Orleans Inspector General Ed Quatrevaux Addresses Tammany's IG Task Force," *Times-Picayune*, September 10, 2013.

45. This approach to funding is now recommended in the Association of Inspectors General's model legislation, (AIG 2002). Association of Inspectors General, "Model Legislation for the Establishment of Offices of Inspector General," 2002, accessed July 9, 2019, http://inspectorsgeneral.org/files/2011/01/IG-Model-Legislation.pdf.

46. Palm Beach County, Florida, Office of Inspector General Ordinance § 2009-049 (2009).

47. Palm Beach County, Florida, Ethics Regulation § 2010-019 (2010).

48. Town of Gulf Stream et al., "Complaint for Declaratory Relief, Filed in the Circuit Court for the 15th Judicial Circuit in and for Palm Beach County, Florida," (2011), accessed July 7, 2019, http://www.pbcgov.com/oig/lawsuit.htm.

49. Palm Beach County, Florida, § 2010-019.

50. Palm Beach County, Florida, § 2010-019.

51. "Order Denying Motion to Intervene," Palm Beach County, Florida, § 2010-019, accessed July 11, 2019, http://www.pbcgov.com/oig/lawsuit.htm.

52. M. Smith, "Daniels Misuses RV, Democrats Charge," *Journal Gazette*, July 22, 2005.

53. Smith, "Daniels."

54. J. Nesbitt, "Daniels Is Cleared on His Use of RV1," *Evansville Courier & Press*, August 2, 2005.

55. Niki Kelly, "Capital Changes: Inspector General Begins Fight on Fraud," *Fort Wayne (IN) Journal Gazette*, July 4, 2005.

56. Niki Kelly, "Ex-State Employee Collects '05 Travel Pay," *Journal Gazette*, 2007.

57. Associated Press, "Former Indiana Lottery Director Cleared of Ethics Charges," Lotterypost.com, August 24, 2007.

58. Associated Press, "Former Indiana."

59. Associated Press, "Former Indiana."

60. Mark Konkol, "Attorney Who Defended County Is New Watchdog—Fought Shakman Hiring Suit," *Chicago Sun-Times*, September 17, 2008.

61. Mark Konkol, "Inspector General Pick Likely Has 2 Key Foes—Watchdog, Anti-Patronage Crusader May See Conflict If Prosecutor Hired," *Chicago Sun-Times*, September 6, 2008; Rob Olmstead, "Frustrated Official Seeks to Jumpstart Search Process," *Arlington Heights (IL) Daily Herald*, March 16, 2008.

62. Rob Olmstead, "Cook County Gets Closer to Having an Inspector General," *Arlington Heights (IL) Daily Herald*, June 27, 2008.

63. Olmstead, "Cook County."

64. F. Spielman, "Alderman Hints Council Inspector's Days Numbered," *Chicago Sun-Times*, September 4, 2013.

65. Spielman, "Alderman Hints."

66. Spielman, "Alderman Hints."

67. Bill Ruthhart and Hal Dardick, "Alderman Pushes through Watchdog Limits Week after Being Probed," *Chicago Tribune*, July 30, 2014.

68. Ruthhart and Dardick, "Alderman Pushes."

69. Hal Dardick, "Chicago Aldermen Reduce Oversight of Their Campaign Fundraising," *Chicago Tribune*, July 30, 2014.

70. David Ress, "Wilder Lashes out at City Auditor—Mayor Angered by Report that Says Security Codes for Gas Cards not in Place," *Richmond Times-Dispatch*, September 3, 2008.

71. Ress, "Wilder Lashes Out."

72. W. Jones, "City Auditor's Work Won't Be as Publicized," *Richmond Times-Dispatch*, October 4, 2009.

73. "City Government: Buried," *Richmond Times-Dispatch*, October 9, 2009.

74. An Act Repealing Legislative Oversight by the Inspector General, Conn. H.R. 6742, sec. 7876–7877 (May 19, 1987).

75. Conn. H.R. 6742; An Act Repealing Legislative Oversight by the Inspector General, Conn. H.R. 6742, testimony of Senator Smith (May 27, 1987).

76. Tim Carpenter, "KanCare Inspector General's Past Shaped by DUI, Bankruptcy, Ethics Woes," *Topeka Capital-Journal*, May 31, 2014.

77. Tim Carpenter, "New KDHE Inspector General Blocked from Official Duties," *Topeka Capital-Journal*, June 5, 2014.

78. Tim Carpenter, "KanCare Inspector General Resigns Amid Questions," *Topeka Capital-Journal*, June 6, 2014.

79. Carol D. Leonnig, "Probe: DHS Watchdog Cozy with Officials, Altered Reports as He Sought Top Job," *Washington Post*, April 24, 2014.

80. Leonnig, "Probe," para. 2.

81. Confidential personal communication, October 10, 2013.

82. Personal communication #17, July 24, 2013.

83. Personal communication #17.

84. Personal communication #21, July 25, 2013.

85. Personal communication #20, July 25, 2013.

86. Massachusetts Office of the Inspector General Act of 1980, Ann. Laws Mass., GL ch. 12A § 2 (2013).

87. Massachusetts Special Commission Concerning State and County Buildings, "Final Report."

88. Virginia Office of the State Inspector General Act, Va. Code Ann. § 2.2-307, et seq. § 2.2-311 (2013).

89. Confidential personal communication, 2013.

90. Confidential personal communication.

91. Minnesota Department of Human Services Office of Inspector General, "Office of Inspector General 2013 Session Overview," 2013, http://www.dhs.state.mn.us/main /groups/licensing/documents/pub/dhs16_177977.pdf.

92. Minnesota Child Care Provider and Recipient Fraud Investigations, Minn. Stat. § 245E.01 (2013).

93. Chicago, Illinois, Office of Inspector General, "Frequently Asked Questions," 2018, https://igchicago.org/about-the-office/frequently-asked-questions/.

94. Hal Dardick and John Byrne, "Aldermen Pick New York Lawyer to Be Watchdog on a Leash," *Chicago Tribune*, November 9, 2011.

95. Dardick and Byrne, "Aldermen Pick."

96. Personal communication #13, July 23, 2013; personal communication #14, July 23, 2013; personal communication #18; personal communication #19, July 25, 2013; personal communication #24, July 26, 2013.

97. Personal communication #18.

98. Personal communication #18.

99. Confidential personal communication, July 23, 2013; personal communication #14.

100. Personal communication #19.

101. Personal communication #19.

102. Personal communication #22, July 26, 2013.

103. Personal communication #24.

104. Personal communication #9, July 3, 2013; personal communication #19.

105. Chicago Board of Education, Inspector General Resolution § 03-0423-RS20 (2003).

106. Indiana Inspector General Act of 2005, Burns Ind. Code Ann. § 4-2-7 (2013).

107. Personal communication #8, May 29, 2013; personal communication #9; per-

sonal communication #11, July 22, 2013; personal communication #14; personal communication #20; personal communication #26, July 30, 2013; personal communication #33, October 17, 2013; personal communication #35, November 5, 2013.

108. Personal communication #9.

109. Personal communication #8; personal communication #9.

110. See, e.g., Colorado Department of Corrections Administrative Regulation § 300-20 (2009); Chicago Board of Education Inspector General Resolution.

111. See, e.g., the Massachusetts OIG's website at http://www.mass.gov/ig/; the website for the office of the executive inspector for the agencies of the Illinois governor at http://www2.illinois.gov/oeig/Pages/default.aspx; the website of the OIG for the city of Chicago, Illinois, at http://chicagoinspectorgeneral.org/; and the New Orleans, Louisiana, OIG's website at http://www2.illinois.gov/oeig/Pages/default.aspx.

112. Chicago, Illinois, Office of Inspector General "Frequently asked questions."

113. See, e.g., Office of Executive Inspector General for the Agencies of the Illinois Governor, "Illinois ethics matters," May 23, 2014.

114. Personal communication #25, July 26, 2013; personal communication #35.

115. Confidential personal communication, 2013.

116. Association of Inspectors General, "Principles and Standards for Offices of Inspector General [Green Book]" (Philadelphia, PA: AIG, 2014), 5. Hereafter referred to as the Green Book.

117. Personal communication #16, July 24, 2013.

118. Personal communication #12, July 22, 2013; personal communication #25; personal communication #27, July 31, 2013.

119. Personal communication #25.

120. Personal communication #9.

121. Personal communication #23, July 26, 2013.

122. See, e.g., Jeremy Olson, Brad Schrade, and Glenn Howatt, "Day Care Threat," *Star Tribune*, July 15, 2012.

123. Minnesota Department of Human Services, Office of Inspector General, "Office of Inspector General 2013 Session Overview."

124. Personal communication #31, October 13, 2013.

125. Personal communication #32.

126. Personal communication #17.

127. Personal communication #14.

128. Personal communication #13.

129. Personal communication #19.

130. Personal communication #24.

131. Personal communication #18.

132. Personal communication #26.

133. Personal Communication #29, October 10, 2013.

134. Personal communication #31.

135. Personal communication #34, October 30, 2013.

136. Personal communication #35.

137. Personal communication #37.

138. Personal communication #13; personal communication #14; personal communication #27.

139. Personal communication #11.

140. Personal communication #24.

141. Personal communication #25.

142. Personal communication #20.

143. Personal communication #23.

144. Personal communication #24.

145. Personal communication #14.

146. Personal communication #23; personal communication #27; personal communication #28, July 31, 2013; personal communication #31.

147. Personal communication #20; personal communication #18.

148. Association of Inspectors General, Green Book.

149. Personal communication #35.

150. Personal communication #35.

151. Personal communication #20; personal communication #27; personal communication #35.

152. Personal communication #27; Virginia Attorney General Opinion §12–076 (2013).

153. Associated Press, Indiana State Wire, "Lawmakers seek review of inspector general office," August 8, 2013.

154. Personal conversation #18, July 25, 2013; personal conversation #20, July 25, 2013; personal conversation #23, July 26, 2013; personal conversation #25, July 26, 2013; personal conversation #25.

155. Personal conversation #26, July 30, 2013.

156. Personal communication #7, June 18, 2012; personal communication #17; personal communication #18; personal communication #20; personal communication #27, personal communication #39, November 7, 2013.

157. Minnesota Department of Human Services, Office of Inspector General, "Office of Inspector General 2013 Session Overview."

158. Personal communication #18.

159. Personal communication #17; personal communication #18; personal communication #19; personal communication #29; personal communication # 37, November 6, 2013.

160. "Inspector General Institute" information page of the Association of Inspectors General website, 2019, accessed July 11, 2019, http://inspectorsgeneral.org/insti tutes/institute/.

161. "Inspector General Institute" information page.

162. "Inspector General Institute" information page.

163. Personal communication #17; personal communication #19; personal communication # 37.

164. Personal communication #34.

165. Association of Inspectors General, Green Book.

166. Association of Inspectors General Training Conference, 2013.

167. Personal communication #35.

168. Association of Inspectors General Training Conference, Long Beach, California, 2008.

169. Association of Inspectors General Training Conference, 2013.

170. Carpenter, *The Forging of Bureaucratic Autonomy.*

CHAPTER 5. CONCLUSION: ARE OFFICES OF INSPECTOR GENERAL EMPTY SYMBOLS OR ENGINES OF ACCOUNTABILITY?

1. John W. Meyer and Brian Rowan, "Institutionalized Organizations: Formal Structure as Myth and Ceremony," *American Journal of Sociology* 83, no. 2 (1977): 340–363.

2. Melvin J. Dubnick and H. George Frederickson, *Public Accountability: Performance Measurement, the Extended State, and the Search for Trust* (Dayton, OH: Kettering Foundation, 2011).

3. John W. Kingdon and James A. Thurber, *Agendas, Alternatives, and Public Policies*, vol. 45 (Boston, MA: Little, Brown, 1984).

4. Murray Jacob Edelman, *The Symbolic Uses of Politics* (Chicago, IL: University of Illinois Press, 1985).

5. James G. March and Johan P. Olsen, *Democratic Governance* (New York: Free Press, 1995).

6. Daniel P. Carpenter, *The Forging of Bureaucratic Autonomy: Reputations, Networks, and Policy Innovation in Executive Agencies, 1862–1928*, vol. 78 (Princeton, NJ: Princeton University Press, 2001).

7. David Osborne and Ted Gaebler, *Reinventing Government: How the Entrepreneurial Spirit Is Transforming the Public Sector* (Kearny, NY: Plume, 1993).

APPENDIX D. DIAGNOSTICS FOR THE EVENT HISTORY ANALYSIS AND COX PROPORTIONAL HAZARDS MODEL

1. Paul D. Allison, *Survival Analysis Using SAS: A Practical Guide* (Cary, NC: SAS Institute, 2010).

BIBLIOGRAPHY

Adcox, S. "Inspector General's Reports Shows SC Agency Tasked with Addressing Racial Inequities Lacks Leadership." *Augusta Chronicle*, August 9, 2015.

Allison, Graham T., and Philip Zelikow. *Essence of Decision: Explaining the Cuban Missile Crisis*. Boston: Little, Brown, 1971.

Allison, Paul D. *Survival Analysis Using SAS: A Practical Guide*. Cary, NC: SAS Institute, 2010.

An Act Creating a State Inspector General. Connecticut H.R. Res. 5090, Testimony of Representative Baronian (May 29, 1985).

———. Testimony of Representative Scully (May 29, 1985).

———. Testimony of Representative Torpey (May 29, 1985).

An Act Creating a State Inspector General. Connecticut S. Res. 5090, Testimony of Senator Larson (June 4, 1985).

An Act Repealing Legislative Oversight by the Inspector General. Connecticut S. Res. 6742 (May 27, 1987).

Ann. Laws Mass. § 16V, GL ch. 6A (2013).

Apaza, Carmen R. *Integrity and Accountability in Government: Homeland Security and the Inspector General*. Abingdon, VA: Routledge, 2016.

Ashworth, Rachel, George Boyne, and Rick Delbridge. "Escape from the Iron Cage? Organizational Change and Isomorphic Pressures in the Public Sector." *Journal of Public Administration Research and Theory* 19, no. 1 (December 2007): 165–187.

Associated Press. "Blagojevich Proposes Changes to Head off Toll Increases." *Mattoon (IL) Journal Gazette*, November 15, 2002. http://jg-tc.com/news/blagojevich-proposes-changes-to-head-off-toll-increases/article_f3f48205-83aa-548d-83a5-9476aefc0045.html/.

———. "Former Indiana Lottery Director Cleared of Ethics Charges." *Lottery Post*, August 24, 2007.

Associated Press, Illinois State Wire. "Judge: Inspector Can Investigate Elective Offices." *Chicago Sun-Times*, January 16, 2014.

Associated Press, Indiana State Wire. "Lawmakers Seek Review of Inspector General Office." *The Dubois County (IN) Herald*, August 8, 2013.

Association of Inspectors General. "About." About Page of the Association of Inspectors General Website. 2019. Accessed June 30, 2014. www.inspectorsgeneral.org.

———. "Inspector General Institute." Association of Inspectors General Website. Updated 2019. http://inspectorsgeneral.org/institutes/institute/.

———. "Model Legislation for the Establishment of Offices of Inspector General." Model Legislation PDF, August 8, 2002. Accessed July 16, 2019. http://inspectorsgeneral.org/files/2011/01/IG-Model-Legislation.pdf.

———. *Principles and Standards for Offices of Inspector General* [Green Book]. Association of Inspectors General, 2nd rev, May 2014. Accessed July 16, 2019. http://inspectorsgeneral.org/files/2014/11/AIG-Principles-and-Standards-May-2014-Revision-2.pdf.

Association of Inspectors General Training Conference, Clearwater Beach, FL, Fall 2012.

Association of Inspectors General Training Conference, Columbus, OH, Spring 2008.

Association of Inspectors General Training Conference, New Orleans, LA, Fall 2013.

Baker, John R. "Exploring the 'Missing Link': Political Culture as an Explanation of the Occupational Status and Diversity of State Legislators in Thirty States." *Western Political Quarterly* 43, no. 3 (1990): 597–611.

Baldacci, Larry. "Edgar Sets Up an Overseer for DCFS Personnel." *Chicago Sun-Times,* April 30, 1993.

———. "3-Year Record of Disaster in Making-Documents Trace the Tragedy of Slain 3-Year-Old." *Chicago Sun-Times,* May 3, 1993.

Balla, Steven J. "Interstate Professional Associations and the Diffusion of Policy Innovations." *American Politics Research* 29, no. 3 (2001): 221–245.

Baumgartner, Frank R., Bryan D. Jones, and Peter B. Mortensen. "Punctuated-Equilibrium Theory: Explaining Stability and Change in Public Policy Making." In *Theories of the Policy Process,* edited by Paul A. Sabatier and Christopher M. Weible, 59–103. Boulder, CO: Westview Press, 2014.

Behn, Robert D. *Rethinking Democratic Accountability.* Washington, DC: Brookings Institution Press, 2001.

Berry, Frances Stokes, and William D. Berry. "State Lottery Adoptions as Policy Innovations: An Event History Analysis." *American Political Science Review* 84, no. 2 (1990): 395–415.

Bibby, John F., and Thomas M. Holbrook. "Parties and Elections." In *Politics in the American States: A Comparative Analysis,* edited by Virginia Gray, Russell L. Hanson, and Thad Kousser, 62–99. Washington, DC: CQ Press, 2017.

Bogert, Nick. "Chicago's New Inspector General a 'Watch Kitten'?" *Examiner,* 2010.

Boushey, Graeme. *Policy Diffusion Dynamics in America.* Cambridge, UK: Cambridge University Press, 2010.

Bovens, Mark. "Analysing and Assessing Accountability: A Conceptual Framework." *European Law Journal* 13, no. 4 (2007): 447–468.

———. "Two Concepts of Accountability: Accountability as a Virtue and as a Mechanism." *Accountability and European Governance,* 28–49. Abingdon, VA: Routledge, 2014.

Bovens, Mark, Thomas Schillemans, and Paul T. Hart. "Does Public Accountability Work? An Assessment Tool." *Public Administration* 86, no. 1 (2008): 225–242.

Box-Steffensmeier, Janet M., and Bradford S. Jones. *Event History Modeling: A Guide for Social Scientists.* Cambridge, UK: Cambridge University Press, 2004.

Boylan, Richard T., and Cheryl X. Long. "Measuring Public Corruption in the American States: A Survey of State House Reporters." *State Politics & Policy Quarterly* 3, no. 4 (2003): 420–438.

Briggs, M. "Mental Patient Abuse Probe Set—Report Alleges Sex Attacks, Beatings." *Chicago Sun-Times*, September 8, 1986.

BuGay, Diane. "Ounce of Prevention." *Chicago Tribune*, June 6, 1993. http://articles .chicagotribune.com/1993–06–06/news/9306060248_1_inmate-implants-preg nancies.

Butler, Alexander W., Larry Fauver, and Sandra Mortal. "Corruption, Political Connections, and Municipal Finance." *The Review of Financial Studies* 22, no. 7 (2009): 2873–2905.

Carpenter, Daniel P. *The Forging of Bureaucratic Autonomy: Reputations, Networks, and Policy Innovation in Executive Agencies, 1862–1928.* Princeton, NJ: Princeton University Press, 2001.

Carpenter, Tim. "KanCare Inspector General Resigns Amid Questions." *Topeka Capital-Journal*, June 6, 2014.

———. "KanCare Inspector General's Past Shaped by DUI, Bankruptcy, Ethics Woes." *Topeka Capital-Journal*, May 31, 2014.

———. "New KDHE Inspector General Blocked from Official Duties." *Topeka Capital-Journal*, June 5, 2014.

Chicago, Illinois, Legislative Inspector General City Ordinance, ch. 2–55 (2013).

Chicago, Illinois, Office of Inspector General City Ordinance, ch. 2–56 (1989).

Chicago Board of Education. Inspector General Resolution, § 03–0423-RS20 (2003).

"Chicago Is Ready for Reform." *Chicago Sun-Times*, July 2, 1989.

"City Government: Buried." *Richmond Times-Dispatch*, October 9, 2009.

Clerk of the Circuit Court and Comptroller, Pinellas County, Florida, Division of Inspector General. "Fraud, Waste, and Abuse Policy." 2019.

Clift, Bob. "Capture the Synergy." Florida Department of Transportation Office of Inspector General Examiner. March 3, 2014. http://fdotoig.wordpress.com/2014/03 /03/capture-the-synergy/.

Cohen, Michael D., James G. March, and Johan P. Olsen. "A Garbage Can Model of Organizational Choice." *Administrative Science Quarterly* 17, no. 1 (1972): 1–25.

Colorado Department of Corrections. Administrative Regulation No. 300-20 (2009).

———. "Office of the Inspector General." Colorado Official State Web Portal. Accessed March 19, 2013. http://www.doc.state.co.us/office-inspector-general.

Colorado Legislative Council Staff. "Concerning the Clarification of the Responsibilities of Investigative Positions within the Department of Corrections." Committee Hearing LLS 99-0746. February 22, 1999.

Colorado Rev. Stat. (CSR) 16-2.5-134 (2013).

Colorado Rev. Stat. (CSR) 17-1-103.8 (2013).

Colorado Senate Judiciary Committee: Hearing on HB 1317, Concerning the Clarification of the Responsibilities of Investigative Positions within the Department of Corrections. April 5, 1999.

Comlossy, M. "Fighting Medicaid Fraud." *State Legislatures Magazine.* National Conference of State Legislatures Website. April 2013. Accessed July 11, 2019. http://www.ncsl.org/research/health/fighting-medicaid-fraud-sl-magazine.aspx#The Defining Differences.

Cook County, Illinois, Office of Independent Inspector General Ordinance, § 2-281 through 2-293 (2013).

"Council Fears Inspector General's Bite." *Chicago Tribune,* September 18, 1989.

Daley, Dorothy M., and James C. Garand. "Horizontal Diffusion, Vertical Diffusion, and Internal Pressure in State Environmental Policymaking, 1989–1998." *American Politics Research* 33, no. 5 (2005): 615–644.

Dardick, Hal. "Chicago Aldermen Reduce Oversight of Their Campaign Fundraising." *Chicago Tribune,* July 30, 2014.

Dardick, Hal, and John Byrne. "Aldermen Pick New York Lawyer to Be Watchdog on a Leash." *Chicago Tribune,* November 9, 2011.

"Day-Care Threat." Series. *Star Tribune,* 2012–2013. http://www.startribune.com/the-day-care-threat/370203871/.

Deslatte, Melinda. "Inspector General Asks Senators to Keep His Office." Associated Press, May 17, 2012.

DiMaggio, Paul J., and Walter W. Powell. "The Iron Cage Revisited: Institutional Isomorphism and Collective Rationality in Organizational Fields." *American Sociological Review* (1983): 147–160.

Dold, R. Bruce. "No Child Deserves This Boy's Pitiful Life." *Chicago Tribune,* May 24, 1996.

Donovan, Lisa. "Berrios Rejects Subpoena." *Chicago Sun-Times,* October 16, 2012.

Dubnick, Melvin J., and H. George Frederickson. "Introduction: The Promises of Accountability Research." *Accountable Governance: Problems and Promises.* Abingdon, VA: Routledge, 2014.

———. *Public Accountability: Performance Measurement, the Extended State, and the Search for Trust.* Dayton, OH: Kettering Foundation, 2011.

Dubnick, Melvin J., and Justin O'Brien. "Rethinking the Obsession: Accountability and the Financial Crisis." *Accountable Governance: Problems and Promises.* Abingdon, VA: Routledge, 2014.

Duehren, Andrew. "U.S. Government Watchdog Reports Faults in DHS Migrant Family Separation Policy." *Wall Street Journal,* October 2, 2018.

Duncan, Ian. "Report: Baltimore retirement fund board chair recruited business partner to oversee $1.6 billion in investments." *Baltimore Sun,* October 4, 2018.

Edelman, Lauren B., Christopher Uggen, and Howard S. Erlanger. "The Endogeneity of Legal Regulation: Grievance Procedures as Rational Myth." *American Journal of Sociology* 105, no. 2 (1999): 406–454.

Edelman, Murray Jacob. *The Symbolic Uses of Politics.* Champaign: University of Illinois Press, 1985.

Elazar, Daniel Judah. *American Federalism: A View from the States.* New York: Crowell-Collier Publishing Company, 1985.

Epp, Charles R. *Making Rights Real: Activists, Bureaucrats, and the Creation of the Legalistic State*. Chicago, IL: University of Chicago Press, 2010.

Erikson, Robert S., Gerald C. Wright, and John P. McIver. "Public Opinion in the States: A Quarter Century of Change and Stability." *Public Opinion in State Politics*: 229–253. Stanford, CA: Stanford University Press, 2006.

Erwin, Barry. "So Why Is It Louisiana Doesn't Need an Inspector General?" Center for Public Integrity Website. May 25, 2012. Updated November 21, 2015. https://public integrity.org/state-politics/commentary-so-why-is-it-louisiana-doesnt-need-an -inspector-general/.

"Events Leading to Ryan's Indictment." *Chicago Tribune*, 2019. http://www.chicagotri bune.com/news/local/breaking/chi-031218ryanevents-graphic,0,6347012.graphic.

Featherly, Kevin. "New DHS Inspector General Kerber Aims to Root Out Fraud, Client Abuse." *Minnesota Lawyer*, November 16, 2011.

Ferguson v. Patton, 985 N.E.2d 1000 (December 14, 2013).

Final Bill Analysis. Florida H.R. Res. 1385 (2014). http://www.myfloridahouse.gov/Sec tions/Documents/loaddoc.aspx?FileName=h1385z.GVOPS.DOCX&DocumentTy pe=Analysis&BillNumber=1385&Session=2014.

Finer, Herman. "Administrative Responsibility in Democratic Government." *Public Administration Review* 1, no. 4 (1941): 335–350.

———. "Better Government Personnel." *Political Science Quarterly* 51, no. 4 (1936): 569–599.

Florida Inspector General Act of 1994. *Florida* Stat. § 20.055 (2013).

Friedrich, Carl J. "Public Policy and the Nature of Administrative Responsibility." *Public Policy* (1940): 3–24.

Frumkin, Peter, and Joseph Galaskiewicz. "Institutional Isomorphism and Public Sector Organizations." *Journal of Public Administration Research and Theory* 14, no. 3 (2004): 283–307.

"Future of Ethics Reform in the Hands of the Governor." *Mattoon (IL) Journal Gazette*, June 9, 2003.

Gerber, Thomas. "Mental Home Abuse Probe Set—State Study Cites Faulty Reporting." *Chicago Sun-Times*, August 27, 1987.

Glick, Henry R., and Scott P. Hays. "Innovation and Reinvention in State Policymaking: Theory and the Evolution of Living Will Laws." *Journal of Politics* 53, no. 3 (1991): 835–850.

Gordon, Sanford C. "Assessing Partisan Bias in Federal Public Corruption Prosecutions." *American Political Science Review* 103, no. 4 (2009): 534–554.

Hardy, Thomas. "Sawyer, Daley Take Spotlight in Mayor's Race." *Chicago Tribune*, January 8, 1989.

Hicks, Josh. "Dozens of Inspectors General Say Federal Agencies Hindering Oversight." *Washington Post*, August 6, 2014.

Illinois Department of Human Services, Office of Inspector General. "History of OIG." DHS About OIG Webpage. http://www.dhs.state.il.us/page.aspx?item=29412.

Illinois Department of Human Services Act. 20 ILCS 1305/1-17 (2013).

———. "Office of the Inspector General (OIG)." DHS Administration Webpage. http://www.dhs.state.il.us/page.aspx?item=29410.

Illinois Executive Ethics Commission and Executive Inspectors General Act of 2006. 5 ILCS 430/20 (2013).

Illinois Executive Order No. 3 (2003).

Illinois Toll Highway Inspector General. 605 ILCS 10/8.5 (2013).

Indiana Executive Order No. 05–03 (2005).

Indiana Inspector General Act of 2005. Burns Ind. Code Ann. § 4-2-7 (2013).

"In Memory of Joseph Wallace." *Chicago Tribune*, April 21, 1993.

"Inspector General." Editorial. *Evansville Courier & Press*, March 20, 2005.

Inspector General Act of 1978. Pub. L. No. 95–452; 5 U.S.C. App. (2010).

Inspector General Authority Improvement Act of 2010. H.R. Res. 5815, 111th Cong. (2009–2010).

Jefferson Parish, Louisiana. Home Rule Charter §4.09 (2013).

Johnson, Charles A., Kathryn E. Newcomer, and Angela Allison. *Balancing Independence and Positive Engagement: How Inspectors General Work with Agencies and Congress.* Washington, DC: IBM Center for the Business of Government, 2015.

Jones, W. "City Auditor's Work Won't Be as Publicized." *Richmond Times-Dispatch*, October 4, 2009.

Jun, Kyu-Nahm, and Christopher Weare. "Institutional Motivations in the Adoption of Innovations: The Case of E-Government." *Journal of Public Administration Research and Theory* 21, no. 3 (2010): 495–519.

"Justice and Amanda Wallace." *Chicago Tribune*, June 22, 1996.

Kaplan, J. "Daley Inspector Denied a Key Power." *Chicago Tribune*, September 13, 1989.

Karch, Andrew. *Democratic Laboratories: Policy Diffusion among the American States.* Ann Arbor: University of Michigan Press, 2007.

Kass, John. "Silence Painful as Koschman's Mom Speaks." *Chicago Tribune*, December 4, 2012.

Kelly, Niki. "Capital Changes: Inspector General Begins Fight on Fraud." *Fort Wayne (IN) Journal Gazette*, July 4, 2005.

———. "Ex-State Employee Collects '05 Travel Pay." *Journal Gazette*, 2007.

Kempf, Robin, J. "Crafting Accountability Policy: Designing Offices of Inspector General." *Policy and Society* 34, no. 2 (2015): 137–149.

Kingdon, John W., and James A. Thurber. *Agendas, Alternatives, and Public Policies.* Boston, MA: Little, Brown, 1984.

Klarner, Carl. "Other Scholars' Competitiveness Measures." Harvard Dataverse, V1. Accessed July 2, 2019. https://doi.org/10.7910/DVN/QSDYLH.

Konkol, Mark. "Attorney Who Defended County Is New Watchdog—Fought Shakman Hiring Suit." *Chicago Sun-Times*, September 17, 2008.

———. "Inspector General Pick Likely Has 2 Key Foes—Watchdog, Anti-Patronage Crusader May See Conflict If Prosecutor Hired." *Chicago Sun-Times*, September 6, 2008.

Koppell, Jonathan G. S. "Pathologies of Accountability: ICANN and the Challenge of 'Multiple Accountabilities Disorder.'" *Public Administration Review* 65, no. 1 (2005): 94–108.

Korecki, Natasha. "Feds Seize Computers, Files on Chicago Officials from Outgoing Inspector General." *Politico*, November 16, 2015.

———. "2 Parties Back Proposal for Toll Authority Inspector." *Arlington Heights (IL) Daily Herald*, January 31, 1997.

Lawrence, M. "State Acts on Patient Abuse—Mental Health Crackdown Today." *Chicago Sun-Times*, August 26, 1987.

Leonaitis, M. "How Long Must Children Pay the Price?" *Chicago Sun-Times*, May 23, 1993.

Leonnig, Carol D. "Probe: DHS Watchdog Cozy with Officials, Altered Reports as He Sought Top Job." *Washington Post*, April 24, 2014.

Levy, Daniel C. "How Private Higher Education's Growth Challenges the New Institutionalism." *New Institutionalism in Education* (2006): 143–162.

Light, Paul C. *Monitoring Government: Inspectors General and the Search for Accountability.* Washington, DC: Brookings Institution Press, 2011.

Longmire, K. "How Long Must Children Pay the Price?" *Chicago Sun-Times*, May 23, 1993.

Louisiana Office of the State Inspector General Act of 2008. La. R.S. 49:220.21 (2013).

"Lynching of Joseph: Suddenly the State Decides It Gives a Damn About Tortured Kids." *Journal Star*, May 16, 1993.

March, James G., and Johan P. Olsen. *Democratic Governance.* New York: Free Press, 1995.

Massachusetts Office of Inspector General. "Inspector General of Massachusetts." Official Webpage. http://www.mass.gov/ig/.

Massachusetts Office of the Inspector General Act of 1980. Ann. Laws Mass., GL ch. 12A (2013).

Massachusetts Special Commission Concerning State and County Buildings. "Final Report to the Massachusetts General Court of the Special Commission Concerning State and County Buildings." Vol. 1. Boston: The Commission, 1980.

McFadden, Robert D. "Billie Sol Estes, Texas Con Man Whose Fall Shook Up Washington, Dies at 88." *New York Times*, May 14, 2013.

McWhirter, Cameron, and Andrew Gottesman. "Good Luck to You, Mother." *Chicago Tribune*, May 9, 1993.

Merriner, J., and L. Rotenberk. "Daley Asks Anti-Corruption Office." *Chicago Sun-Times*, January 31, 1989.

Meyer, Heinz-Dieter. "The Rise and Decline of the Common School as an Institution: Taking 'Myth and Ceremony' Seriously." *The New Institutionalism in Education* (2006): 51–66.

Meyer, John W., and Brian Rowan. "Institutionalized Organizations: Formal Structure as Myth and Ceremony." *American Journal of Sociology* 83, no. 2 (1977): 340–363.

Millard, E. "Stop Finger-Pointing Over Child's Death." *Chicago Sun-Times*, May 21, 1993.

Minnesota Child Care Provider and Recipient Fraud Investigations. Minn. Stat. § 245E.01 (2013).

Minnesota Department of Human Services. "DHS Announces Creation of the Office of Inspector General." Webpage. August 18, 2011. http://www.dhs.state.mn.us /main/idcplg?IdcService=GET_DYNAMIC_CONVERSION&dID=119547.

———. "Organization/Management." Webpage. Updated February 8, 2019. http:// www.dhs.state.mn.us/main/idcplg?IdcService=GET_DYNAMIC_CONVERSION &RevisionSelectionMethod=LatestReleased&dDocName=id_000261.

Minnesota Department of Human Services, Office of Inspector General. "Office of Inspector General 2013 Session Overview." 2013. http://www.dhs.state.mn.us/main /groups/licensing/documents/pub/dhs16_177977.pdf.

Minn. HF 2256 (2010).

Minn. HF 3047 (2010).

Minn. HF 4049 (2008).

Minn. HF 4119 (2008).

Mintrom, Michael. "Policy Entrepreneurs and the Diffusion of Innovation." *American Journal of Political Science* (1997): 738–770.

Mohr, Lawrence B. "Determinants of Innovation in Organizations." *American Political Science Review* 63, no. 1 (1969): 111–126.

Moore, J. "McCaskill Drafting New IG Bill with Focus on Small Agencies." Federal News Network, April 10, 2014.

Morris, L. "On the Road to Reform—Gov.-Elect Daniels Realized the State Needs Not Just Mechanisms, but the Right Attitude." *Fort Wayne (IN) News-Sentinel*, December 28, 2004.

Moynihan, Donald P. "Learning Under Uncertainty: Networks in Crisis Management." *Public Administration Review* 68, no. 2 (2008): 350–365.

Nesbitt, J. "Daniels is cleared on his use of RV1." *Evansville Courier & Press*, August 2, 2005.

Newcomer, Kathryn E. "The Changing Nature of Accountability: The Role of the Inspector General in Federal Agencies." *Public Administration Review* (1998): 129–136.

———. "Opportunities and Incentives for Improving Program Quality: Auditing and Evaluating." *Public Administration Review* (1994): 147–154.

Newcomer, Kathryn, and George Grob. "Federal Offices of the Inspector General: Thriving on Chaos?" *American Review of Public Administration* 34, no. 3 (2004): 235–251.

New Orleans, Louisiana, Office of Inspector General. La. Ord. § 2-1120 (2006).

New Orleans, Louisiana, Office of the Inspector General. "OIG: New Orleans Office of Inspector General." Webpage. 2014. http://www.nolaoig.gov/.

"Notes and Quotes from the Louisiana Legislature." Associated Press, Louisiana State Wire, May 7, 2012.

Novak, Tim, and Chris Fusco. "State's Attorney Blocks Probe of Her Office—Who Killed David Koschman? A Watchdog's Investigation." *Chicago Sun-Times*, May 5, 2011.

Office of Inspector General, Chicago Board of Education. "Annual Report." 2013. http://www.cps.edu/About_CPS/Departments/Documents/OIG_FY_2013_Annu alReport.pdf.

Office of Inspector General, City of Chicago. "Department: Office of the Legislative Inspector General." https://igchicago.org/.

———. "Frequently Asked Questions." Webpage. Revised 2018. https://igchicago.org /about-the-office/frequently-asked-questions/.

Office of the Executive Inspector General for the Agencies of the Illinois Governor. "Illinois ethics matters." A Newsletter from the Office of Executive Inspector General for the Agencies of the Illinois Governor. May 23, 2014. https://www2.illinois.gov /oeig/Documents/Newsletter_May_23_2014.pdf.

Olmstead, Rob. "Cook County Gets Closer to Having an Inspector General." *Arlington Heights (IL) Daily Herald*, June 27, 2008.

———. "Frustrated Official Seeks to Jumpstart Search Process." *Arlington Heights (IL) Daily Herald*, March 16, 2008.

———. "Inspector General Ordinance Stalls Again." *Arlington Heights (IL) Daily Herald*, June 12, 2007.

Olson, Jeremy, Brad Schrade, and Glenn Howatt. "Day Care Threat." *Star Tribune*, July 15, 2012.

Ortiz, L. "Phelan Unsure of Need for Inspector Job." *Chicago Sun-Times*, April 8, 1993.

Osborne, David, and Ted Gaebler. *Reinventing Government: How the Entrepreneurial Spirit Is Transforming the Public Sector*. New York: Plume, 1993.

Pacheco, Julianna. "The Social Contagion Model: Exploring the Role of Public Opinion on the Diffusion of Antismoking Legislation Across the American States." *Journal of Politics* 74, no. 1 (2012): 187–202.

Pallasch, Abdon M. "County Board OKs Hiring Watchdog: Commissioners Vote to Settle Shakman Suit." *Chicago Sun-Times*, November 30, 2006.

Palm Beach County, Florida, Office of Inspector General. Fl. Ord. No. 2009-049 (2009).

———. Fl. Ord. No. 2010-019 (2010).

———. "Lawsuit Regarding Inspector General Founding." 2019. http://www.pbcgov .com/oig/lawsuit.htm.

———. "Office of Inspector General Palm Beach County." Webpage. 2013. http:// www.pbcgov.com/oig/.

"Past Problems with Inspectors General Cloud Blagojevich Ethics Plan." *Journal Gazette*, November 3, 2003.

Patterson, Steve. "New County Fraud-Fighter Wants to Beef Up Staff." *Chicago Sun-Times*, May 26, 2004.

———. "Watchdog for County Corruption OKd—But Stroger Must Find Money for It." *Chicago Sun-Times*, July 25, 2007.

"Peace Comes to Amanda Wallace." *Chicago Tribune*, August 5, 1997.

Pew Charitable Trusts, The. "Infographic: S&P State Credit Ratings, 2001–2012." Stateline Article. The Pew Charitable Trusts, July 13, 2013. http://www.pewtrusts.org

/en/research-and-analysis/blogs/stateline/2012/07/13/infographic-sp-state-credit
-ratings-20012012.

Phillips, Frank. "Weld stripping watchdogs of bite, critics say." *Boston Globe*, April 2, 1991.

Pollitt, Christopher. "Performance Blight and the Tyranny of Light?" In *Accountable Governance: Problems and Promises*, edited by Melvin J. Dubnick and H. George Fredrickson. Abingdon, VA: Routledge, 2014.

Project on Government Oversight. "Inspectors General: Many Lack Essential Tools for Independence." February 26, 2008. http://www.pogo.org/our-work/reports/2008 /go-ig-20080226.html#Budget_Line_Items_and_Transparency.

Purdue University, Office of the President. "Mitchell E. Daniels Jr. Biography." Personal biography. 2019. Accessed July 1, 2019. https://www.purdue.edu/president /about/biography.php.

Putnam, Robert D. *Bowling Alone: The Collapse and Revival of American Community*. New York: Simon and Schuster, 2001.

Ranney, Austin. "Parties in State Politics." *Politics in the American States: A Comparative Analysis*. Boston: Little, Brown, 1971.

"Reformers Hope Ryan Indictments Resurrect Ethics Legislation." *Journal Gazette*, April 8, 2002.

Ress, David. "Wilder Lashes Out at City Auditor—Mayor Angered by Report That Says Security Codes for Gas Cards Not in Place." *Richmond Times-Dispatch*, September 3, 2008.

Rhoden, R. "New Orleans Inspector General Ed Quatrevaux Addresses Tammany's IG Task Force." *The Times-Picayune*, September 10, 2013.

Richmond, Virginia, Office of Inspector General. Va. Func. Div. 7, § 2-230, et seq. (2008).

Roeper, Richard. "Is It Ever Proper to Take Someone's Birth Right?" *Chicago Sun Times*, May 3, 1993.

———. "Power-Grabbing Governor Soon Will See Error of His Ways-Blagojevich Wants to Set Up a Super Inspector General." *Chicago Sun-Times*, June 21, 2003.

Rogers, E. M. *Diffusion of Innovations*. 5th ed. New York: Free Press, 2003.

Romzek, Barbara S., and Melvin J. Dubnick. "Accountability in the Public Sector: Lessons from the Challenger Tragedy." *Public Administration Review* (1987): 227–238.

Ruthhart, Bill, and Hal Dardick. "Alderman Pushes through Watchdog Limits Week After Being Probed." *Chicago Tribune*, July 30, 2014.

"Sabotaging tollway reform." *Beacon News*, September 4, 2003.

S&P Global. "U.S. Local Governments' General Obligation Ratings: Methodology and Assumptions." Webpage. September 12, 2013. https://www.standardandpoors. com/en_US/web/guest/ratings/ratings-criteria/-/articles/criteria/governments/fil ter/us-public-finance.

Saulny, Susan. "Portrait of a Politician: Vengeful and Profane." *New York Times*, December 10, 2008.

Schmadeke, Steve. "Daley Nephew Vanecko Pleads Guilty in Koschman Death." *Chicago Tribune*, February 1, 2014.

Schmidt, Michael S., and Mike Apuzzo. "Hillary Clinton Emails Said to Contain Classified Data." *New York Times*, July 24, 2015.

Schmidt, William E. "Man in the News; Chicago Mayor from a New Mold; Richard Michael Daley." *New York Times*, April 5, 1989.

Scott, W. Richard. "The Adolescence of Institutional Theory." *Administrative Science Quarterly* (1987): 493–511.

———. "Institutions and Organizations: Toward a Theoretical Synthesis." In *Institutional Environments and Organizations: Structural Complexity and Individualism*, edited by W. Richard Scott and John W. Meyer, 55–80. Thousand Oaks, CA: SAGE, 1994.

Seidel, Jon. "Cook County Inspector Taking Berrios to Court." *Chicago Sun-Times*, June 12, 2013.

Selznick, Philip. *Leadership in Administration: A Sociological Interpretation*. New Orleans, LA: Quid Pro Books, 2011.

Sfondeles, Tina. "Game of Thrones? Watchdog Sees 'Scheme to Defraud' in Pritzker Toilet Tax Break." *Chicago Sun-Times*, October 1, 2018.

Shaffer, C. "Cleveland Will Create Police Inspector General as Part of Justice Department Reform." Cleveland.com, May 26, 2015.

Sharkansky, Ira. "The Utility of Elazar's Political Culture: A Research Note." *Polity* 2, no. 1 (1969): 66–83.

Shipan, Charles R., and Craig Volden. "Policy Diffusion: Seven Lessons for Scholars and Practitioners." *Public Administration Review* 72, no. 6 (2012): 788–796.

Simon, Herbert A. "On the Concept of Organizational Goal." *Administrative Science Quarterly* (1964): 1–22.

Simpson, Dick, James Nowlan, Thomas J. Gradel, Zmuda, Melissa Mouritsen, David Sterrett, and Douglas Cantor. "Chicago and Illinois, Leading the Pack in Corruption." Chicago, IL: University of Illinois at Chicago, Department of Political Science and Institute for Government and Public Affairs, 2012. http://www.uic.edu/depts/pols/ChicagoPolitics/leadingthepack.pdf.

Smith, M. "Daniels Misuses RV, Democrats Charge." *Journal Gazette*, July 22, 2005.

Spielman, F. "Alderman Hints Council Inspector's Days Numbered." *Chicago Sun-Times*, September 4, 2013.

Stone, Deborah A. *Policy Paradox and Political Reason*. Glenview, IL: Scott Foresman, 1988.

Sweeney, Annie. "Feds Seek 15-, 20-Year Sentence for Blagojevich." *Chicago Tribune*, December 1, 2011.

"The System Is the Scapegoat." *Chicago Tribune*, October 29, 1993.

Tarrant, K. "Random musings: A Tale of Two I.G.'s and Other Contemplations." *Examiner*, 2013.

"Thanks, Aldermen." Editorial. *Chicago Tribune*, April 13, 2010.

"3-Year-Old Joseph's Death Was a Tragedy of Errors." Editorial. *State Journal-Register*, May 10, 1993.

Town of Gulf Stream et al. "Complaint for Declaratory Relief, filed in the Circuit Court for the 15th Judicial Circuit in and for Palm Beach County, Florida." 2011. http://www.pbcgov.com/oig/lawsuit.htm.

United States Census. "2010 Annual Survey of Public Employment and Payroll." Webpage. 2010. http://www.census.gov//govs/apes/historical_data_2010.html.

———. "2010 Census Summary File 1, Table P1 Total Population." Webpage. 2010. Accessed Sept. 22, 2015. http://factfinder.census.gov.

United States Department of Justice. "Report to Congress on the Activities and Operations of the Public Integrity Section." Webpage. 2005. Accessed November 15, 2013. http://www.justice.gov/criminal/pin/.

———. "Report to Congress on the Activities and Operations of the Public Integrity Section." Webpage. 2006. Accessed November 15, 2013. http://www.justice.gov/criminal/pin/.

———. "Report to Congress on the Activities and Operations of the Public Integrity Section." Webpage. 2007. Accessed November 15, 2013. http://www.justice.gov/criminal/pin/.

———. "Report to Congress on the Activities and Operations of the Public Integrity Section." Webpage. 2008. Accessed November 15, 2013. http://www.justice.gov/criminal/pin/.

———. "Report to Congress on the Activities and Operations of the Public Integrity Section." Webpage. 2009. Accessed November 15, 2013. http://www.justice.gov/criminal/pin/.

———. "Report to Congress on the Activities and Operations of the Public Integrity Section." Webpage. 2010. Accessed November 15, 2013. http://www.justice.gov/criminal/pin/.

———. "Report to Congress on the Activities and Operations of the Public Integrity Section." Webpage. 2011. Accessed November 15, 2013. http://www.justice.gov/criminal/pin/.

———. "Report to Congress on the Activities and Operations of the Public Integrity Section." Webpage. 2012. Accessed November 15, 2013. http://www.justice.gov/criminal/pin/.

United States House of Representatives, Committee on Oversight and Government Reform. *Inspectors General: Independence, Access and Authority*, ser. no. 114-4. Washington, DC: U.S. Government Printing Office, 2015.

United States Military Academy. "History of the U.S. Army Inspector General." Accessed June 21, 2019. https://westpoint.edu/about/west-point-staff/inspector-general/history.

"Victimization of Joshua Wallace." *Chicago Tribune*, May 17, 1995.

Virginia Attorney General Opinion. Va. 12–076 (July 19).

Virginia Office of the State Inspector General Act. Va. Code Ann. § 2.2-307, et seq. (2013).

Volden, Craig. "States as Policy Laboratories: Emulating Success in the Children's Health Insurance Program." *American Journal of Political Science* 50, no. 2 (2006): 294–312.

Walker, Jack L. "The Diffusion of Innovations Among the American States." *American Political Science Review* 63, no. 3 (1969): 880–899.

Weyland, Kurt. *Bounded Rationality and Policy Diffusion: Social Sector Reform in Latin America*. Princeton, NJ: Princeton University Press, 2009.

"What about Joshua?" *Chicago Tribune*, April 20, 1994.

"What Went Wrong in the Courtroom." *Chicago Tribune*, May 2, 1993.

Wong, D. S., and Don Aucoin. "House OK's 31.5% Raise for Inspector General." *Boston Globe*, April 16, 1997.

Yasutake, Seiichi Michael. "Sensitive Treatment." *Chicago Tribune*, August 17, 1994.

Zernike, Kate, and W. K. Rashbaum. "Port Authority Investigating New Jersey Lane Closing." *New York Times*, December 10, 2013.

INDEX